SCOTT FORESMAN

SF

EXPRESS

SECOND EDITION

John Ruszkiewicz
University of Texas at Austin

Maxine Hairston
University of Texas at Austin

Christy Friend
University of South Carolina

Prentice Hall

Upper Saddle River   London   Singapore
Toronto   Tokyo   Sydney   Hong Kong   Mexico City

Editorial Director: *Leah Jewell*
Executive Editor: *Paul Crockett*
Assistant Editor: *Jennifer Conklin*
Editorial Assistant: *Tara Culliney*
Marketing Director: *Brandy Dawson*
Marketing Manager: *Emily Cleary*
Marketing Assistant: *Kara Pottle*
VP/Director of Production and Manufacturing: *Barbara Kittle*
Production Editor: *Maureen Benicasa*
Production Assistant: *Marlene Gassler*
Copyeditor: *Deborah Prato*
Permissions Coordinator: *Ron Fox*
Text Permission Specialist: *Michael Farmer*
Prepress & Manufacturing Manager: *Nick Sklitsis*
Prepress & Manufacturing Assistant Manager: *Mary Ann Gloriande*
Web/Media Production Manager: *Lynn Pearlman*
Senior Media Editor: *Christy Pepper*

Creative Design Director: *Leslie Osher*
Art Director: *Anne Nieglos*
Interior & Cover Design: *Michelle Wiggins*
Director, Image Resource Center: *Melinda Reo*
Manager, Cover Visual Research and Permissions: *Karen Sanatar*
Manager, Rights and Permissions: *Zina Arabia*
Manager, Visual Research: *Beth Brenzel*
Image Permission Coordinator: *Debbie Hewiston*
Cover Art: *Getty Images/PhotoDisc*
Typeface: *10/12 Adobe Garamond*
Composition: *Interactive Composition Corporation*
Printer/Binder: *RRDonnelley & Sons*
Cover Printer: *Phoenix Color Corporation*

This book includes 2009 MLA guidelines.

Credits and acknowledgments borrowed from other sources and reproduced, with permission, in this textbook appear on pages 249–250.

Library of Congress Cataloging-in-Publication Data

Ruszkiewicz, John J.,
    SF express / John Ruszkiewicz, Maxine Hairston, Christy Friend. — 2nd ed.
      p. cm.
    Includes index.
    ISBN 0-205-75120-2
        1. English language—Rhetoric—Handbooks, manuals, etc. 2. English language—Grammar—Handbooks, manuals, etc. 3. Report writing—Handbooks, manuals, etc. I. Hairston, Maxine. II. Friend, Christy. III. Title.
    PE1408.R8685 2006
    808'.042—dc22   2004060228

10 9 8 7 6 5 4 3

Prentice Hall
is an imprint of

www.pearsonhighered.com

ISBN 10:   0-205-75120-2
ISBN 13: 978-0-205-75120-4

Contents

Photo Credits

Preface

DRAWING FROM THE BEST-SELLING COMPREHENSIVE HANDBOOK, *The Scott Foresman Handbook for Writers,* this new, second edition of *SF Express* covers all the basics of grammar, mechanics, usage, and punctuation. But it does much more. Like its predecessor, this edition of *SF Express* is designed to help writers working in new environments with fresh attitudes toward composing. The fact is most of us are composing more and faster than ever before—in both our professional and personal lives. This means we sometimes require general advice, sometimes we want precise guidelines, and sometimes we need to know where to go for more detailed information. You'll find all these needs addressed in this book.

This new edition offers several new features:

- **Chapter 1, "Critical Reading and Viewing"** now encompasses critical reading of visual images and multimedia as well as traditional, printed texts. We've added new information to keep pace with changing classroom environments.

- **Chapter 5, "Making Arguments," created especially for this edition,** offers concise guidelines for analyzing and writing persuasive arguments for academic and public audiences.

- **A new section in Chapter 10 defines "academic honesty"** to remind writers that this concept should inform their research processes from the moment they choose a topic until they hand in the final version of a paper.

Though we've made significant updates, this edition retains what readers told us they need and appreciate most in *SF Express.* We still provide a concise, up-to-date introduction to doing research in college and documenting work in professional styles (MLA, APA, Chicago, and CSE). A complete student paper provides a clear model of MLA style.

■ *Express!* boxes at the beginning of each chapter provide strategies for writing, thinking, and research. Specific guidelines and rules, amplified by numerous hand-edited examples, then follow.

■ *E-tips,* thoroughly updated for this edition, cover everything from using Web search engines to choosing background

colors for Web sites. To be sure writers have all the information they need, each chapter in the second edition also includes
■ *Destinations boxes list* Web sites that cover topics in especially
comprehensive or creative ways. The URL for each *Destination* is
accompanied by an explanation of its content.

Writers sometimes need a little encouragement or humor
so each chapter begins with a comment on writing, research, or
creativity by people as different as Albert Einstein and David
Letterman. Thumbnail portraits of each commentator give this
handbook a human face.

All of this material is presented in the friendly and encour-
aging style that has been a hallmark of SF handbooks for more
than a decade. We hope you enjoy this second edition of *SF
Express*.

JOHN RUSZKIEWICZ
MAXINE HAIRSTON
CHRISTY FRIEND

PART ONE

Writing and Thinking

1 Critical Reading and Viewing

"Be careful what you swallow. Chew!"
—GWENDOLYN BROOKS, poet

If you want to participate in a democratic society, you will need to sharpen your ability to think critically. As a student and as a citizen, you are bombarded each day with written and visual messages that try to influence you—to buy a cell phone, to donate money to a certain charity, to vote for one candidate instead of another. In college, you will learn to sharpen your abilities to assess these messages. You will learn to read analytically, listen carefully, ask questions, challenge statements, and consider how new information fits into what you already know. The analytic and problem-solving skills you learn in college will serve you for the rest of your life.

In college, you're often dealing with complex issues, using information from books, articles, and Internet sources. Thus, an important part of becoming a critical thinker is becoming a critical reader.

Yet, the visual media you encounter convey equally complex ideas, drawing on eye-catching images, charts, or other graphic devices to appeal to readers. Because such images are so ingrained in our everyday lives, it's important to know how to approach them critically, how to "read" them just as carefully as we read printed words. These critical viewing skills are called *visual literacy.*

Critical reading and viewing involve cultivating an attitude of inquiry, of asking the right questions so you can make informed decisions about what you see rather than letting it control *you*.

a Ask Questions

When you're doing research, whether it's for buying a car or gathering data for a term paper, ask the journalists' questions about the texts and images you find: Who? What? Why? Where? When?

- *Who* created this and what are the author's credentials?
- *What* kind of text is this? Is it an academic article, a political poster, a documentary film? What is the text's message or argument?

- *Why* was this text or image created?
- *Where* did it first appear?
- *When* did it first appear?

Then reflect on the answers to these questions. For example, judge the expertise of an author: A professional basketball coach might be an expert on motivation but not a credible source in a debate on welfare reform. Think about what interests or biases may be concealed by an organization's name. What reputation does the organization have? Who are the people behind the organization? Weigh your sources, and verify any information that seems to serve their special interests.

b Evaluate the Evidence

Evaluate the evidence an author presents. In academic writing, evidence should be solid, verifiable, and factual. Ask whether the evidence is substantial.

- How much evidence is presented? Is it enough to prove the author's case?
- Where did the evidence come from? Are the sources credible, relevant, and up to date?
- How much of the evidence is anecdotal? How much is hearsay?
- Is all the evidence fully and fairly presented? If not, what information has been left out?

Evaluate, too, whether the writer's claims are fully supported by the evidence presented. Be especially skeptical when a source proposes a simple solution to a complex problem.

EXPRESS!

It's especially important to assess the evidence in a text when it's presented visually in a chart, table, or graph. Numbers themselves don't lie, but they can be presented in misleading ways. For example, the two graphs that follow present exactly the same data on unemployment rates in the United States. Figure 1.1, however, appears to show a sharp drop in the rate, whereas in Figure 1.2 the decrease looks insignificant because it is plotted on a grid with a wide range of rates, from 0 to 100 percent of the population. In this case, the creator of the second graph has misled readers by including numbers on the scale that aren't typically part of this phenomenon (even though it's technically possible to have 100 percent unemployment, the rate in the United States has rarely been below 4 percent or above 11 percent).

Figure 1.1

Figure 1.2

c Assess Visual Elements

The "body language" of a text—the way a page is laid out and the choice of visual elements such as color, images, font, and headings—can strongly influence readers' responses to its message. When you look at a document that includes visual elements, ask yourself these questions.

- *What ideas and information are emphasized and what is downplayed?* Boldface or large type, bright colors, or placement near the top of a page are just a few of the ways that writers highlight ideas.
- *What formatting devices has the writer used?* Borders, headings, columns, and other devices for arranging information can reveal important clues about the genre and intended audience for a document.
- *How do illustrations, photographs, or other images add to the document's message?* Sometimes images add information or context that's not provided in accompanying text. At other times, images may reveal something about the values, opinions, or biases of the author.

These two political posters, created during different wars (World War II and Vietnam) in different eras, illustrate how visual elements can be combined in different ways to suggest different arguments. During World War II, Rosie the Riveter symbolized civilian support for the war effort. The Vietnam poster, however, employed very different visual elements to send a contrary message.

 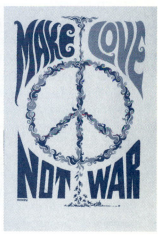

d Talk Back to the Text

Critical reading is an active process. To get the most from your reading, don't rely strictly on highlighting—talk back to the text.

- *Use your own words.* When you arrive at an important point or get tangled in a difficult passage, translate it into your own words to clarify its meaning.

- *Track the structure.* Notes can also help you follow a text's structure. At crucial transitions, jot down a key word or two that explains where the ideas are going or how a new point fits in—"Example 3," for instance.
- *Respond with* your *ideas.* Don't just accept what the text says; talk back. Does a proposal excite or anger you? Write "Yes!" or "Bad logic." If the text raises questions, write them down: "But what about . . . ?" This kind of dialogue helps you develop your own perspective on the issues being raised.

e | Summarize

The best way to make sure you've understood any text is to write a summary: a boiled-down restatement of its content in your own words. A summary can help you study and review important reading material in your classes. If you are writing about research, you can summarize material that supports your thesis but doesn't contain information you need to share in detail with your readers (see pages 62–63).

The length of your summary will depend on how you will use it. A summary may restate only the thesis of an article in a single sentence, or it may present the gist of a whole text, its major arguments and important examples.

- Restate the thesis in a sentence or two, using your own words.
- Divide the text into its major sections, and compose a sentence that sums up the content of each.
- Put the pieces together. Begin with the author and title of the piece, followed by your restatement of the thesis. Then add your summaries of each major section in order.
- Revise and polish. If others will read your summary, add transitions so the piece reads smoothly, and eliminate any repetitions and minor details. Don't mix in your own opinions; keep the author's ideas and your own clearly separated.

If you use any source material word for word, be sure to place this quoted material within quotation marks.

<DESTINATIONS>

For two excellent online guides to evaluating Web sites, visit the Sonoma State University Library at <http://libweb.sonoma.edu/assistance/eval.html> and the Sheridan

Libraries of the Johns Hopkins University at
<http://www.library.jhu.edu/researchhelp/general/evaluating/index.html>.

For information about critically viewing mass media, visit the
Center for Media Literacy at <http://medialit.org>.

For comprehensive checklists on how to analyze written
information, visit the Cornell University Library at
<http://www.library.cornell.edu/okuref/research/skill26.htm>. ■

2 The Writing Situation

*"Writing saved me from the sin and
inconvenience of violence."*
—ALICE WALKER, novelist

Writing is not a purely academic skill that you will leave behind at graduation. On the contrary, the writing skills you learn in
college will help you participate more effectively in the world. In
our information-based society, almost everyone writes. Through
writing, people exchange information, debate issues, promote
their own values, and advocate change. Alice Walker alludes to the
power of writing in the quotation at the beginning of this chapter.
Writing affects people's beliefs and lives, and it can change the way
a society or organization operates. Writing is also an important
medium for intellectual inquiry. Many people use writing to work
through their ideas on an issue or to help organize complicated
material they learn at school or on the job.

Every writing situation differs, and thus there is no secret
formula for writing well. Nevertheless, you will almost always
write in response to some specific situation. Analyze your writing
situation by asking yourself these three basic questions.

- What do I want to say?
- To whom?
- Why?

Probably no other single habit will do more to help you become a
skilled writer.

EXPRESS!

Some writing situations are defined, at least in part, by others—a letter to the editor may have a word limit imposed by the newspaper, a business memo must provide certain information requested by a manager. In your classes, the verbs your instructors use in assignments give you important clues about the types of responses they expect. Because these verbs describe patterns of thinking that can be applied to many situations, they are a helpful guide to actions you can take in writing both in and away from school.

Analyze: break an argument or concept into parts and explain the relationships among them; evaluate; or explain your interpretation or judgment.

Apply: take a concept, formula, or theory and adapt it to another situation.

Argue, prove: take a position on an issue and provide reasons and evidence to support that position.

Compare: point out similarities between two or more concepts or situations.

Contrast: point out differences between two or more concepts or situations.

Critique, evaluate: make and support a judgment about the worth of an idea, theory, or proposal, accounting for both strengths and weaknesses.

Define: state a clear, precise meaning for a concept or object, and perhaps give illustrative examples.

Discuss, explain: offer a comprehensive presentation and analysis of important ideas on a topic, supported with examples and evidence.

Review, summarize: briefly lay out the main points of a larger theory or argument.

Trace: explain chronologically a series of events or the development of a trend or idea.

a | Topic

Whether you are assigned a subject or choose one yourself, consider your own interests and questions to decide on a specific topic and approach.

- What does the assignment ask you to do? Make sure you fulfill its requirements.
- If you are writing for a college course, what specific aspect of the general course content do you find interesting? For any piece of writing, what interests you about the topic? What makes you curious? Why?

- What do you know a good deal about? What do you enjoy reading or arguing about? What community issues do you find compelling?

b Purpose

When you're planning a paper, think about your specific goals.

- Do you want to inform, persuade, or entertain readers?
- How do you want readers to respond? Do you want them to react intellectually, emotionally, or both? Do you hope to get them to agree with you, consider your new ideas, or join your cause?
- Do you want readers to take action? If so, have you made clear what you think they should do?

c Audience

To write effectively, analyze the knowledge, experience, and beliefs of your readers. Then tailor your work to appeal to them.

- Who wants or needs to know more about your topic?
- Is your audience a small, specific group or a more general one? What do you know about them?
- What interests the members of this audience? What is important to them?
- How much do they already know about your topic? What new information do they need? What questions will they have?
- Will any of your points conflict with their current beliefs or perceptions? How can you persuade them to consider a new point of view?
- What kinds of examples and evidence will they find effective and convincing? How much support should you provide?
- What tone of voice should you use—formal or informal?

d Genre

Audiences tend to approach different types of writing with different expectations. Each type of writing, or *genre*, whether it be a lab report for a biology course, an editorial for the school paper, an essay for your English class, or a home page for the World Wide Web, follows specific rules, patterns, or conventions. You must understand the conventions of the genre you're writing for to reach your audience and achieve your purpose.

- What form should your paper take to reach your audience and fulfill your purpose? Will you write a letter, editorial, research paper, news article, essay, memo, email message, Web page, or other genre?
- Where could you publish this paper?
- Why do people read this type of paper? To be educated? Stimulated? Challenged? Entertained?
- What features or organization will readers expect?
- What style will readers expect? Breezy slang? Formal sentences?
- If this is a paper for expert readers, is there specialized language you should use? If the paper is for a general audience, how can you help readers understand unfamiliar ideas or difficult terms?
- Are there guidelines or samples you can consult?

Examine an effective sample of the genre to see how it is organized. An essay for a humanities course, for example, often includes an introduction that states the thesis, a supporting body that expands on the introduction, and a conclusion that sums up what the paper has achieved. A business report may require an executive summary that lays out the main points and conclusions of the paper, a description of the problem, a proposed solution, and a discussion of budget and feasibility. A Web site probably includes an opening screen that conveys introductory information concisely, hyperlinks to other pages that include short chunks of additional information, and links to other, external Web sites that are organized for easy navigation.

<DESTINATION>

For advice, templates, and links for writing letters to the editor, letters to legislators, editorials, press releases, and news articles, visit <http://home.comcast.net/~garbl/writing/action.htm>. ∎

3 Planning

"Writing is easy; all you do is sit staring at a blank sheet of paper until drops of blood form on your forehead."
                    —GENE FOWLER, journalist and
                                         biographer

An hour or two of planning can save you days of writing on an unproductive topic. Finding a topic that will interest both you and your readers, focusing the topic to make it manageable given your time and length limitations, and developing a tentative thesis to direct your research and thinking are valuable preliminaries to drafting a writing project.

EXPRESS!

Some of the best issues for writing are unfolding right in front of you. Perhaps your school board is debating whether to require uniforms in city high schools. Or a branch of your town's library that serves a low-income neighborhood is slated for closure. Or local politicians are trying to figure out the best way to regulate the use of firearms by police officers. Because such debates affect your everyday life, you're bound to have a strong interest in their outcome. And when you concentrate on local events, expert sources of information—newspapers, community organizations, government offices, and interested citizens—are close at hand. Should you decide to publish your writing outside the classroom, you may even directly influence public opinion.

a Find a Topic

Be good to yourself. Choose an interesting topic, one that won't bore you. If possible, select one you already have some knowledge and ideas about.

List some possibilities. Begin by listing some broad possibilities—as many as you can think of—that sound promising.

Think in threes. What three subjects do you like to read about—in magazines, newspapers, books, on the Web? What three do you know the most about—topics you often discuss, questions others seek your advice about? What three subjects are you most curious about? What three do you most enjoy arguing about? What three issues in your community do you care about the most?

Next, run through your list quickly to reject topics if they seem too broad or if you may not be able to find enough material about them.

Choose two or three ideas that seem both manageable and interesting. Talk with friends or classmates; they may see angles that haven't occurred to you or point out problems you didn't anticipate.

Browse online and offline. If you don't have a subject yet, try browsing in the periodicals room or the new book section for topics that spark your curiosity. Look up your subject in the library catalog, computer database, or the directory of the Library of Congress (better known as the *Subject List*) to expand your ideas.

Don't limit your browsing to print and database sources. The Internet offers a multitude of resources and ideas for writing. If you have a general subject already, look for newsgroups to see what others are saying about it, and check for listservs you can subscribe to or whose archives are open for browsing by the public. If you still need a subject, browse the subject categories in *Yahoo!* on the World Wide Web; if you have one, try several different keyword searches, using a search engine such as *AltaVista* or *About.com,* to see which aspects of your topic seem worth exploring further. For more on online sources, see pages 55–58.

b Focus Your Topic

Learn to write more about less. It's the details—the particular people and events—that will make your material come alive for readers and help you treat your subject more thoroughly. Instead of writing a piece on single parenthood, for example, you might narrow your topic to the difficulties of being an unmarried teen parent. Better yet, focus on whether providing day-care centers in high schools can help teenage mothers graduate and support their children.

Focus your topic by doing some preliminary freewriting, brainstorming, or clustering. Consult a library index related to your topic—for example, the multidisciplinary index *Periodicals*

Abstract or a discipline-specific index such as the *Art Index*. In the index, scan the subcategories of your topic for ways to narrow your focus. To pinpoint specific issues for further investigation, ask yourself questions such as the following.

- *Questions of fact.* What is known about your topic? What still isn't known? Are some "facts" contested? Do facts seem to change with time?
- *Questions of definition.* How do the words you use to define your topic affect your understanding? How do your interpretations of the "facts" fit your topic into a larger category?
- *Questions of value.* Is the idea you'll be writing about a good thing or a bad thing? Ethical or unethical? Worthwhile or not worthwhile? Workable or not workable?
- *Questions of policy.* What should be done? What action should your audience take? Are existing laws and policies effective? What new laws should be passed?

c   Develop a Thesis

An essay's thesis is a sentence (or sometimes two or three sentences) that explicitly identifies the point of the paper or summarizes its main ideas. Your thesis statement is likely to evolve as you conduct research, draft, and revise, but often, writers construct a tentative thesis to help organize a first draft.

A thesis statement makes a claim that might be questioned or challenged. Ask about your thesis, "Does this thesis provoke a reaction? Could someone legitimately disagree with it?" If not, change it. Take a stand. And if an intelligent reader might respond, "So what?" or "Big deal!" sharpen the point you intend to make.

TOO VAGUE

A child who has a computer at home has many educational advantages.

MORE POINTED

Elementary school teachers are worried about the growing gap between children who have computers at home and can play math and reading games and those whose parents cannot afford such advantages for their children.

Ask basic questions about your topic—particularly How? and Why? Get to the heart of a matter in defining a topic. Examine issues that affect people.

LIFELESS

Child abuse is a serious problem with three major aspects: causes, detection, and prevention.

CHALLENGING

Prosecutors in some communities have based charges of child abuse on types of hearsay evidence that are now receiving tougher scrutiny from courts.

Your research will likely lead you to reconsider and limit your original thesis statement. Exactly how you limit it will depend on what your thesis promises. For example, you can consider this commitment in terms of whether you have started with a claim of fact, definition, value, or policy. As your project progresses, you'll want to refine your thesis to make a distinct and limited claim, and then follow through with the appropriate support and evidence.

ORIGINAL CLAIM OF DEFINITION

Zoos promote cruelty to animals.

CLAIM SPECIFIED AND LIMITED BY RESEARCH

Confining large marine mammals in sea parks for public amusement is, arguably, a form of cruelty to animals.

COMMITMENTS

- Find legal/popular definitions of "cruelty to animals."
- Define specific criteria for "cruelty."
- Examine what experts say about the condition of animals in marine parks. Or do fieldwork in such a park.
- Find statistics on animal health in marine parks.
- Find expert opinion on both sides of the issue.
- Show that conditions in marine parks meet (or do not meet) criteria for "cruelty to animals."

e-TIPS

Unlike essays written for college classes, Web sites whose main purpose is to inform the public about an issue may well be organized around a simple listing of related topics:

Child abuse is a serious problem with three major aspects: causes, detection, and prevention.

Focal points such as this statement can work well when you need to divide an issue or idea into its basic components. If you were organizing a Web site around this statement, you would likely make some fairly brief, general statements about the problem of child abuse on the home page. The home page would then link to three separate pages, one for each of the three aspects—causes, detection, and prevention. The simplicity of this design would help make the Web site coherent.

d | Plan Your Project

Most writers need some plan for organizing their ideas. For a short piece of writing, you might make a working list of key points, such as this student of literature did:

```
Thesis: Comic moments in Macbeth emphasize how
disordered the world becomes for the Macbeths
after they murder the king.
1. Comic moments after the murder of King Duncan
2. Comedy at the feast for Banquo
3. Comedy in the sleepwalking scene
4. Conclusion
```

As you think of specific subpoints and examples, you can add them under each of the main points. If you are writing an essay, think in terms of what your readers will need in the introduction, the body, and the conclusion. For more complex projects, consider creating a sentence outline to develop a strong framework for your writing.

e-TIPS

If you are working on a hypertext project with multiple pages, storyboard your piece (see 6a) to help you visualize the entire structure before you start writing. First, make a sketch like this one that shows how the various pages of your hypertext will connect to one another.

Second, sketch the layout of text and graphics for each page. Plan to include at least one element that will be present on every page to cue your readers that they are still in your pages. For example, the bicycle at the top of this page might serve as such an element.

<DESTINATIONS>

For in-depth discussion and numerous examples of how to craft effective thesis statements, visit the Writing Center at the University of North Carolina at Chapel Hill at <http://www.unc.edu/depts/wcweb/handouts/thesis.html>.

For specific examples of how to use clustering and brainstorming to focus your topic, visit the Writer's Web at the University of Richmond at <http://writing2.richmond.edu/writing/wweb/cluster.html>. ■

4 Drafting and Revising

"It's not that the creative act and the critical act are simultaneous. It's more like you blurt something out and then analyze it."
—ROBERT MOTHERWELL, painter and writer

You can accumulate material even before you begin a draft. Start a computer file to store preliminary ideas, notes from your reading, quotations from sources, remarks from discussions, and your tentative conclusions about the topic. Over time you'll accumulate a surprising amount of prose that you can shape into a final text.

When you want to rework a draft, just save your most current draft as a new file with a new version number. Try out each new version while preserving all the work you've already done (you might want to use portions of an earlier version in your final draft).

EXPRESS!

Beginning to write can be difficult, even for professional writers. Authors have described the paralyzing anxiety they sometimes feel as they stare at a blank piece of paper or an empty computer screen. The delay that this fear can cause is so common that it even has a name: *writer's block*. What is the cure for writer's block? "Blurt something out," as Robert Motherwell puts it. Try some of the following ways to get started.

- Jot down a few key phrases: "Talk about yak milk"; "remember to refer to Rodriguez"; "make it clear that sitting in a tree for a year is a noble act."
- Write the same sentence over and over again: "I want to know what to write. I want to know what to write."
- Turn off your computer monitor and just start writing anything that occurs to you about your subject without looking at your words.

At some point, you will feel more relaxed and be able to start writing on your topic.

a | Start Drafting

Experiment with the following strategies for starting a draft. You may find one that seems particularly productive, but even so, knowing several strategies will prove helpful because each project offers unique challenges.

- *Start anywhere.* If you feel most confident about an idea that will likely fall in the middle of the piece, start writing about that point. Don't waste your time agonizing over your opening.
- *Maintain momentum.* Don't criticize your writing or edit your work as you go along. Don't get bogged down in details.
- *Use writing that you did while planning.* You can lift whole sentences out of an outline, for example, and embellish them later when you revise.
- *Keep your readers in mind.* Write as though you are conversing with a member of your audience.
- *Track new ideas.* When you get a flash of insight or think of a telling phrase, jot it down so you'll remember it at the appropriate time.
- *Read to fill in gaps.* You may realize that you don't have enough information on a particular point to proceed. Research it.

b | Explore Your Ideas

Use drafting to explore your ideas. Ideas are not fixed, and sometimes as soon as a writer sees an idea on paper, he or she begins to question it. Write down your questions and your possible responses in order to explore what you think. For example, you might look at an idea and ask, "But what if . . . ?" and then ponder different conditions or settings in which it might or might not be true. This process will help you refine your ideas and may change your tentative thesis statement considerably.

If you've done a lot of planning, you may already have completed much of this process. That's fine; every writer works somewhat differently. However, even a draft based on a detailed outline can go off in a new direction. Allow new ideas to occur to you; evaluate them when you have finished a rough draft.

If you get stuck and don't know what to write next, try various strategies such as freewriting (writing nonstop, even if you write nonsense), brainstorming on your own or with a friend or classmate, or responding to questions such as the following.

- What are some examples of this general idea?
- What is a general idea that might encompass all of these examples or anecdotes?
- What logically connects these two ideas?
- What other ideas does this idea seem to lead to naturally?
- If I believe this idea, what else must I believe?
- How does this relate to my thesis?

Questions such as these are helpful because they lead you to shift your perspective slightly. Often, all you need to get writing again is to examine your idea from a different point of view.

c Write Strong Paragraphs

A strong paragraph is unified, focusing a reader's attention on one main idea. It is coherent, indicating which thoughts go together logically. A powerful paragraph is also well-developed, supplying ample details and explanations to make each point come to life.

Write unified paragraphs.   Individual sentences in a paragraph should not go off in their own separate directions. Every sentence should connect with the others to form a chain or web that keeps the reader focused on a central idea.

A *topic sentence* states this central idea. When the topic sentence comes at the beginning of a paragraph, it often predicts the ideas or supporting examples to come; when it comes at the end, it often sums up the details in a general statement. Here is a unified paragraph that begins with the topic sentence.

> The [Soviet] society in which I had grown up was one that officially proclaimed sexual equality and made it a point of great pride, yet stereotyped men and women in ways reminiscent of the American fifties. At school, we had mandatory home economics for girls and shop for boys, a practice no one thought of challenging. At the music school where my mother taught, to say that someone played "like a girl"—pleasantly, neatly, and without substance—was a commonly used put-down; in literary reviews, the highest compliment to be paid a woman writer or poet was that she wrote like a man.
> —Cathy Young, *Keeping Women Weak*

Not all paragraphs need topic sentences. In reports and analyses, however, topic sentences keep paragraphs on track.

Write coherent paragraphs. Each sentence in a paragraph should clearly relate to the sentences that precede and follow it. Always include a hint, a reference, a hook, or a repetition to help the reader link what you're saying with what has come before and what lies ahead.

Repeating key ideas establishes a motif for a paragraph. In this paragraph, Robert Coles repeats the term *idealism* or *idealists* four times, connecting that concept to the phrase *commitment to reform* in his opening statement.

> I have noticed, again and again, that those youths who are openly troubled about their commitment to reform as against their desire to live comfortable, respectable lives, are the ones who seem to last longest as active **idealists**. . . . Such youths state the obvious about themselves—that they simply cannot or will not shake off a youthful **idealism** in favor of various "practicalities," various "adjustments to reality," as pressed upon them by parents, friends, former college classmates, new acquaintances. Nor are such young **idealists** only to be found in the most prominent places. . . . Any number of dedicated **idealists** straddle the world of commerce and philanthropy, and make a constant and personal effort on behalf of poor people.   —Robert Coles, *The Moral Life of Children*

Transitions—words and phrases that link ideas—help readers understand the connections between sentences.

> If one lives in an affluent suburb, it's easy to get the impression that Americans are healthy. In **such** places, walkers and bicycle riders abound, and restaurants feature low-fat entrees. The truth is, **however,** that many Americans are not healthy. Thirty percent are seriously overweight, alcoholism is a chronic problem, and an increasing number of teenagers are smoking. **Moreover,** obesity among children is increasing rapidly.

TRANSITIONAL TERMS

Similarity: in addition, likewise, moreover, similarly, such, further, furthermore

Contrast: however, instead, nevertheless, although, in spite of, on the other hand, not only, yet

Sequence: after, before, later, now, subsequently, then, hence-
forth, first, second, finally
Cause and effect: as a result, because, consequently, for, since,
therefore, thus
Others: personal pronouns such as *he, she,* and *they*
demonstrative pronouns such as *this, that, these,*
those, and *such*
the relative pronouns *who, which, where,* and *that*

Parallelism—repeated grammatical patterns—is a forceful
device for achieving unity (see pages 144–145). In the paragraph
on Soviet sexism by Cathy Young (page 19), notice the series of
prepositional phrases that begin clauses: "At school," "At the
music school," "in literary reviews." These phrases tighten the
connection between the individual sentences.

Develop the paragraph.   A well-developed paragraph provides
enough reasons and details to make its point clear. This first draft
doesn't.

> Many people claim that they have the right to
> choose whether to wear a motorcycle helmet.
> But they don't consider the negative effects
> of their decisions on their families and the
> public. So mandatory helmet laws are a good
> idea.

In his revision, the writer provides the explanation and evidence to
support his point.

> Many people claim they have the right to
> choose whether to wear a motorcycle helmet.
> In their view, they are the ones who risk
> getting hurt, so why should anyone else care?
> But they don't consider the negative effects
> of their decisions on others. First,
> their families will suffer. According to
> the National Highway Traffic Safety
> Administration, motorcyclists are about
> 20 times more likely to be killed in highway
> accidents than car passengers. As a result,
> wives and husbands are more likely to be left

```
without spouses; and children will be left
without parents. The public will suffer
as well. The public-interest group Advocates
for Highway and Auto Safety cites a study
showing that taxpayers supplied more than
$300,000 per person to provide long-term
care to victims of motorcycle-related brain
injuries; in 1993, motorcycle helmet laws
saved the public more than $500 million in
medical expenses. So in protesting mandatory
helmet laws, motorcycle riders cannot argue
that they're hurting only themselves.
```

d Review Your Draft

When you revise, you are not yet fixing or correcting your writing. Rather, you are shaping a work in progress, reviewing what you have written, and looking for ways to improve it. You may get new ideas and shift the focus of the piece entirely; you may decide to cut, expand, and reorganize on a large scale. At this point, don't tinker. THINK BIG.

- If possible, set the piece aside for a few days before rereading it so you can view it more objectively.
- Review the assignment, as well as any feedback you have received from your instructor and colleagues. Ask yourself frankly how you feel about the paper. What's good that you definitely want to keep? Where does it seem weak?
- Create a simple outline that includes the thesis, the topic sentence or main idea of each paragraph, and the concluding idea. Check this bare-bones structure. First, does the draft hang together logically? If it doesn't, examine your concluding idea. Does it reveal a new intention that you discovered through drafting? You may want to begin with this point in your next draft. Second, consider the audience for your piece. If they read only the outline, would they understand all your main points? Would they understand the significance of these points to your thesis? If not, sketch in what other kinds of information you need to add to make your main points clear and their connection to your thesis obvious.

- Consider now a bold option: Should you write an entirely new draft? Starting a second time from scratch may be easier than repairing a draft that just won't work.

Although some writers like to produce early drafts in longhand, today most college students prefer to compose onscreen. If you compose on a word processor, remember to print out a hard copy when you are ready to revise. Seeing the entire draft on paper gives you a fresh look at your writing and can help you spot areas that need work. Changes that you mark on the hard copy can easily be keyed on your word processing file to produce a new draft.

e | Create a Revision Plan

If you find you have a workable first draft, go through this list systematically to decide what you should revise. As you check each aspect of your writing, take notes on the areas that need improvement and, especially, any specific ideas you have for revising.

PURPOSE

- If someone else read your draft, would he or she immediately understand what you're trying to achieve?
- Did you clearly state in the first paragraph or two what you intend to do?
- Does the draft develop all the main points you intended to make?

AUDIENCE

- Who are your readers? What will they want from your piece?
- Have you covered any material already familiar to your readers?
- Have you left important concepts unexplained or important terms undefined?
- Have you used language your readers will understand?

COMMITMENT

- What exactly did you promise readers at the beginning of the paper? Did you fulfill those promises?
- Did you support all the claims you made in your thesis?
- Does your conclusion agree with your opening?

FOCUS

- Are you generalizing about your topic instead of stating specific positions?
- Have you relied mostly on common knowledge? If so, your piece may lack credibility.
- Have you supported your ideas with sufficient evidence and examples?

ORGANIZATION

- Does your piece focus on a point or state a thesis? Does it then develop that point significantly?
- Do the transitions move readers sensibly from point to point?
- Would the paper work better if you moved some paragraphs around and thus changed your emphasis?

PROPORTIONS

- Are the parts out of proportion? For example, is the beginning much more detailed than the rest?
- Can your readers tell what points are most important by the amount of attention you've given to them?
- Does the paper build toward the most important point?

f Edit and Proofread

When you have a strong second or third draft, you can begin to edit. Editing entails making small-scale changes that involve style, word choice, tone, choice of examples, and arrangement at the sentence level. Consult Chapters 19–24 when you edit.

Proofreading entails checking for punctuation errors, omissions, spelling mistakes, and lapses in standard grammatical usage. Consult Chapters 28–33 for punctuation rules and Chapter 34 for spelling rules.

<DESTINATIONS>

For comprehensive information about each stage of the writing process, visit the *Writer's Web* at the University of Richmond at <http://writing2.richmond.edu/writing/wweb.html>.

For a discussion of topic sentences and paragraph structure, visit the *Writing Tutorial Services* at Indiana University at <http://www.indiana.edu/~wts/wts/paragraphs.html>.

For brief guidelines on how to respond constructively to a class-mate's or colleague's draft, visit the University of Wisconsin-Madison Writing Center's *Writer's Handbook* at <http://www.wisc.edu/writing/Handbook/PeerReviews.html>. ■

5 Making Arguments

"If you can find something that everyone agrees on, it's wrong."
—MO UDALL, former U.S. senator

Many of the writing projects you undertake in college and on the job will ask you to explain and support a position—to make an *argument*. This chapter introduces you to some basic structures and strategies of argument.

a Basic Parts of an Argument

An argument is a claim supported by reasons and evidence. British philosopher Stephen Toulmin has developed a useful model for understanding how arguments are structured.

EXPRESS!

We follow the Toulmin model throughout this chapter because it is a comprehensive, useful, and commonly used way of understanding argument, but your instructor or classmates may use different termi-nology to refer to the basic parts of an argument. Ask your instructor to clarify any confusion you may have about these terms.

This model says that in every argument, a writer begins by making a general assertion—a *claim*—and then produces one or more grounds for supporting that claim. Support for a claim may include *reasons* (smaller assertions that often begin with the word *because*) and *evidence* (relevant examples, facts, statistics, or experts' statements).

Here's a simple way of outlining how an argument is put together.

> **Argument = Claim + Reason(s) and Evidence**

Suppose you're writing an article for your campus magazine on the benefits of working during college. Using Toulmin's model, you might develop your argument as follows.

CLAIM	First-year students at large universities benefit academically from having a job.
REASON	(Because) The social contacts they make at work help them feel less isolated on campus.
EVIDENCE	1. A recent poll conducted by the admissions office found that working students have more friends than students who do not work. 2. My ex-roommate developed a network of friends and study partners while working part time in a campus copy shop.

Arguments rest on general beliefs, or warrants, that are sometimes unstated.

Toulmin's model uses the term *warrant* to describe the justification—a general belief, rule, or principle—that links together the claim and its support in an argument. A persuasive argument must rest on warrants that readers find satisfactory, or readers will reject it.

When you write an argument, you will sometimes need to state the warrant and provide some explanation and support for it. Reasons and evidence used to support the warrant in an argument are called *backing*. Backing is especially important if you suspect that some of your readers disagree with the beliefs that are the bases for your argument. Here's how an argument looks with warrant and backing.

ARGUMENT WITH WARRANT AND BACKING

CLAIM	The federal government should spend more money on cutting-edge cancer research.
REASON/EVIDENCE	Studies show that the treatments developed in this kind of research save lives.
WARRANT	The government has an obligation to fund programs that save lives.

BACKING   The government collects taxes from all citizens, and so it has a responsibility to spend those funds on programs that promote the public's welfare. Thus, programs that protect citizens' lives and health should be a funding priority.

b | Craft Persuasive Arguments

Toulmin's model offers a helpful framework for generating material to include in any writing project that asks you to persuade an audience or argue a point.

State your claim.   Figure out what you want readers to take from your piece: Do you want readers to look at some phenomenon in a new way? Do you want them to be aware of a problem they hadn't noticed before? To hold a particular position on a current issue? To take action? Your answer is your claim.

Gather reasons and evidence.   What material can you find to develop and strengthen your claim? Check the library for books, periodical articles, research reports, and government documents on the topic. Conduct a search for online sources (see Chapters 8–10 for more on finding print and online sources). For expert testimony, consider setting up an interview. Depending on your audience, you might also draw on your own experiences or first-hand knowledge about the topic.

Evaluate your evidence.   No matter where your evidence comes from, be sure that it meets certain basic requirements.

- *Timeliness.* Are the statistics, information, and examples you use recent, or are they so old that they may no longer be accurate?
- *Comprehensiveness.* Do you have enough support for your claim, or are you making generalizations based on one or two examples?
- *Credibility.* Do you draw your evidence from sources that both you and your readers trust?

For a detailed discussion of how to evaluate evidence, see Chapter 9.

c Consider Opposing Viewpoints

When you want your readers to accept your arguments and perhaps act on them, remember that you won't persuade people by making them angry. You'll only make them stick to their positions more stubbornly. For this reason, we suggest that you think of argument not as a battle but as a dialogue. In a dialogue, both sides exchange ideas as they search for a solution. The following section explores strategies for working productively with readers who disagree with you.

Identify shared beliefs and values. Even if you're addressing readers whose position is completely opposed to your own, search for common ground. Any shared belief or value, no matter how general, may serve as a warrant on which you can build an argument those readers will find reasonable. For instance, both proponents and opponents of gun-control legislation value public safety, although they have different ideas about how to achieve it.

Present opposing arguments fairly. If you're going to write about controversial issues, you can't simply pretend that your position is the only one. You'll need to acknowledge that other arguments exist. It is equally important that you learn to describe other positions accurately and respectfully. In doing so, you enhance your own credibility.

d Avoid Logical Fallacies

Critical thinkers learn to recognize *fallacies,* those shoddy imitations of well-reasoned arguments. Most fallacies are flashy shortcuts that look good at first but turn out to be based on dubious assumptions and careless generalizations. Here are ten kinds of fallacy you're likely to encounter frequently.

Avoid argument to the person (in Latin, *ad hominem*). This fallacy makes a personal attack on an opponent rather than focusing on the issue under discussion. *Ad hominem* arguments become smear tactics when a speaker or a writer attacks an opponent's personality or personal life.

Avoid circular reasoning. This fallacy—also called *begging the question*—happens when instead of supporting a claim, the writer simply restates the claim in different words. Take this faulty argument: "We should not raise taxes to build the new airport because doing so would cost taxpayers more money."

Avoid hasty generalizations.
This fallacy involves drawing conclusions from too little evidence.

> It's not safe to travel now because terrorists set off a bomb in the Tel Aviv airport last month, and two weeks later another bomb blew up at Heathrow Airport in London.

Terrorist incidents at two airports do not provide sufficient evidence on which to base a broad claim about travel safety all over the world.

Be careful about making claims that use absolute terms such as *always, never, everyone, no one, all,* and *none.* When you're talking about human events, absolutes are seldom accurate, so cover yourself by using qualifiers like *some, in most cases,* and *many.*

Avoid false cause arguments (in Latin, *post hoc, ergo propter hoc*).
These arguments incorporate the faulty assumption that because one event follows another, the first event caused the second.

> In the years since the highway speed limit was raised to 70 miles per hour, the annual number of traffic fatalities in our state has doubled. Clearly, the new speed limit is causing unnecessary deaths.

Too many factors enter into changes in traffic fatality numbers for such a conclusion to be accepted without further analysis and evidence.

Avoid either/or arguments (also called *false dilemmas*).
This type of faulty reasoning states an argument in terms that imply that one must choose between only two options—right/wrong, good/bad, moral/immoral, and so forth.

> If we allow that factory to come into our town, we are dooming ourselves and our children to a lifetime of breathing filthy air.

Many other options are available between the extremes of no factory and filthy air; one might be to require the factory to install scrubbers to clean its emissions.

A loaded rhetorical question that allows for only one acceptable answer is another form of the either/or argument.

> Are we going to increase the number of police officers in this city, or are we going to abandon it to gangs and drug dealers?

When an arguer tries to force a false dilemma on you, your best response is to challenge your opponent's polarized thinking immediately and point out other alternatives to his or her oversimplified view.

Avoid red herrings. This tactic involves diverting the audience's attention from the main issue by bringing up an irrelevant point. (The phrase refers to the practice of dragging a strong-smelling smoked herring across a trail to confuse hunting dogs and send them in the wrong direction.) For example, a mayor might complain as follows.

> While it may be true that my campaign released inaccurate information about my opponent's voting record, I am clearly just being targeted by a hostile media.

The charges of press bias might be true, but the attitude of the media has no bearing on the official's misbehavior.

Avoid slippery slopes. This fallacy occurs when a writer assumes that taking an initial action will automatically set in motion an unstoppable chain of events.

For instance, a politician who supports funding a new complex to house agencies dealing with homelessness might argue that when homeless people have easy access to services under one roof, they will be able to get the help they need, find jobs, and become productive citizens. Perhaps so, but without explanation and argument to support each link in that chain, these predictions have no solid foundation, and you shouldn't readily accept them.

Avoid false analogies. These are comparisons that do not hold true or prove misleading.

> A corporation couldn't operate without the leadership of a CEO to set priorities and make the big decisions. A family operates the same way: One spouse must be the head of the household, or chaos will result.

Certainly a business and a household share superficial similarities, but the two entities have completely different functions, involve different kinds of interpersonal relationships, and operate according to different value systems (profit and efficiency versus nurturance and loyalty). To assume that what holds true in one environment should hold true in the other is a logical leap that readers won't be willing to take.

Avoid *non sequitur*.   Latin for "it does not follow," this fallacy occurs when writers draw on irrelevant evidence or reasons to support a claim. *Non sequitur* is similar to the red herring fallacy, but whereas red herrings are designed to distract a reader from the central argument, *non sequitur* asks readers to accept the irrelevant material as proof. Here are two examples.

> That candidate would be an excellent mayor—after all, he goes to church every Sunday.

> That can't be a top-notch university. It's in a run-down area surrounded by housing projects and abandoned warehouses.

What does church attendance have to do with being mayor? About as much as being in a bad neighborhood has to do with the quality of faculty and curriculum at a university: that is to say, little.

Avoid bandwagon appeal.   This tactic argues that an activity or a product must be worthwhile because it is popular. Youngsters who try to persuade their parents that they must have a particular brand of sneakers or a new kind of in-line skates because "everybody has them" are using bandwagon tactics. As millions of parents have pointed out, popularity doesn't necessarily guarantee merit.

<DESTINATION>

The Writing Center at the University of North Carolina at Chapel Hill has developed a useful worksheet on identifying logical fallacies. Visit at
<http://www.unc.edu/depts/wcweb/handouts/fallacies.htm>. ■

6 Design

> *"You can have anything you want in life if you dress for it."*
> —EDITH HEAD, costume designer

Design plays an important role in how readers perceive the information contained in any document, whether it is a research paper, a Web site, a church newsletter, a poster, or a résumé. A well-conceived design helps readers get what they need from the screen or printed page.

a Planning

Start by visualizing the entire document as you want it to look, including its color scheme, to create a document that's easy for readers to follow.

Design for an audience and a purpose.   Every design decision should be based on what you know or can assume about your readers, as well as your own purpose for creating the document. What do readers want and need to know? What do they value? What will catch their interest? What is your goal in creating this document?

Decide on the image you want to convey.   Based on your audience and purpose, what personality do you want your document to project? Serious and scholarly? Crisp and direct? Fun-loving? Documents project distinct images to readers. Such images can arise from the tone of the document, from its visuals and layout, and from the attitude and point of view taken by its author(s).

Examine effective models of your genre.   Each genre—research paper, Web site, résumé, and so forth—has its own conventions of format, tone, and style. Refer to effective samples of the genre you are working in to take advantage of elements readers will expect to find.

e-TIPS

Survey your word processor's document templates. These templates follow traditional page layouts, so they provide a great starting place for designing documents, even if you eventually want a customized final product.

Storyboard your project. Storyboarding is a process graphic designers and artists use to visualize an entire project before implementing it. If you're planning a seven-page Web site, take out seven pieces of paper, and, with colored pencils, sketch what you want each of the pages to look like. This process will help you explore how the elements of text and graphics will look in relation to each other. For example, storyboarding allows you to decide on the following.

- whether to use charts and graphs, and where to place them
- whether a newsletter should have two or three columns
- how the layouts of the front and back panels of a brochure will coordinate
- how the headings in a résumé should be laid out to organize your work and educational experiences

b Layout

First impressions matter. You want your document to make a strong first impression, so think about its "body language." Be sure your document doesn't appear crowded or lopsided and that your readers can follow the flow of information easily. Consider the following points.

- Leave plenty of white space in your document—areas where no text or visuals appear.
- Move readers from upper left to lower right—put key information at the upper left, and arrange supporting points so the reader's eye moves smoothly down and across the page.
- Group related information—use headings, lists, and boxes to organize information for your readers.

c Academic Papers

Academic papers follow the conventions of the documentation style used, such as MLA (Chapter 11), APA (Chapter 12), CMS (Chapter 13), and CSE (Chapter 14). For example, MLA style requires the following formatting features.

- one-inch margins at top, bottom, left, and right
- double-spacing throughout, including long quotations and Works Cited list

- author's last name and page number in the upper right corner of every page (see the E-tips below)
- title of the paper, centered, in the same typeface as the rest of the paper
- every figure (picture or illustration) with a caption below it, and a reference within the text of the paper

Getting your name and page number one-half inch from the top of each page while maintaining one-inch margins for your text can be tricky. Fortunately, word processing programs have built-in "header" functions to assist you in getting your headers in the right place on every page. In the "Help" section of your word processing program, look for "headers"; learning to use this function can save you a lot of time and frustration when you're producing your final drafts.

See pages 98–109 for an academic paper formatted in MLA style. Even if your instructor does not require you to follow a particular documentation style, you can use the MLA guidelines to make your paper easy to read.

d   Résumés

Your résumé is a brief outline of your academic and employment history, designed to give a prospective employer an overview of your achievements, skills, work experience, and references. Take great care in preparing your résumé: Assemble accurate information and arrange it handsomely.

Résumés may be printed on paper or posted on the Internet. Companies may also scan résumés electronically to find keywords that indicate that a job candidate has the credentials needed for the available position. When planning your résumé, consult these general tips, but also examine models of résumés to discover which organizational strategies will best suit your résumé (see Figure 6.1).

- Adapt your résumé for each position.
- Use headings and subheadings to organize your presentation.
- *Personal information:* For paper résumés, include your name, current address, and phone number(s), and the electronic address of your Web site, if you have one. For online résumés, include your name, email address, and the address of your

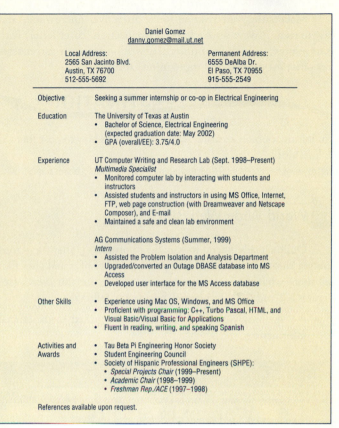

Daniel Gomez
danny.gomez@mail.ut.net

Local Address: Permanent Address:
2565 San Jacinto Blvd.   6555 DeAlba Dr.
Austin, TX 76700   El Paso, TX 70955
512-555-5692   915-555-2549

Objective	Seeking a summer internship or co-op in Electrical Engineering
Education	The University of Texas at Austin • Bachelor of Science, Electrical Engineering (expected graduation date: May 2002) • GPA (overall/EE): 3.75/4.0

Experience	UT Computer Writing and Research Lab (Sept. 1998–Present)
	Multimedia Specialist
	• Monitored computer lab by interacting with students and
	  instructors
	• Assisted students and instructors in using MS Office, Internet,
	  FTP, web page construction (with Dreamweaver and Netscape
	  Composer), and E-mail
	• Maintained a safe and clean lab environment
	
	AG Communications Systems (Summer, 1999)
	Intern
	• Assisted the Problem Isolation and Analysis Department
	• Upgraded/converted an Outage DBASE database into MS
	  Access
	• Developed user interface for the MS Access database

Other Skills	• Experience using Mac OS, Windows, and MS Office • Proficient with programming: C++, Turbo Pascal, HTML, and Visual Basic/Visual Basic for Applications • Fluent in reading, writing, and speaking Spanish

Activities and
Awards
	• Tau Beta Pi Engineering Honor Society
	• Student Engineering Council
	• Society of Hispanic Professional Engineers (SHPE):
	  • *Special Projects Chair* (1999–Present)
	  • *Academic Chair* (1998–1999)
	  • *Freshman Rep./ACE* (1997–1998)

References available upon request.

Figure 6.1 This print résumé emphasizes education and experience.

Web site, if you have one—no phone number or physical address. (By law, you cannot be required to state your age, gender, race, religious or sexual preference, political affiliation, or marital status.)

- *Education:* Specify your academic major and minor and any honors or special recognition you may have received, as well as any course work relevant to the position.
- *Work experience:* List all of your work experiences.
- *References:* Indicate the placement service that has your complete dossier, or list your references at the bottom of your résumé if appropriate.
- *Scannable résumés:* Do not use images, italic or underlined type, unusual fonts, vertical lines, or multiple columns. Use specific nouns that describe your credentials instead of relying on verbs to carry your meaning.

Make sure your résumé looks attractive, uncrowded, and easy to read. Always send a letter of application (cover letter) with your résumé; consult your university writing center or career services office for models and more information.

<DESTINATION>

For information on creating résumés, as well as how to post them online, visit
<http://www.career.uga.edu/students/internetresourcesforthejobhunt.html>. ■

e | World Wide Web Pages

Online, readers tend to scan for information rather than read straight through, so you should provide plenty of visual cues that tell them what is most important in a Web site you create (see Figures 6.2 and 6.3). In general, ensure the following.

- the opening screen is concise and packed with crucial information

Figure 6.2 Home Page

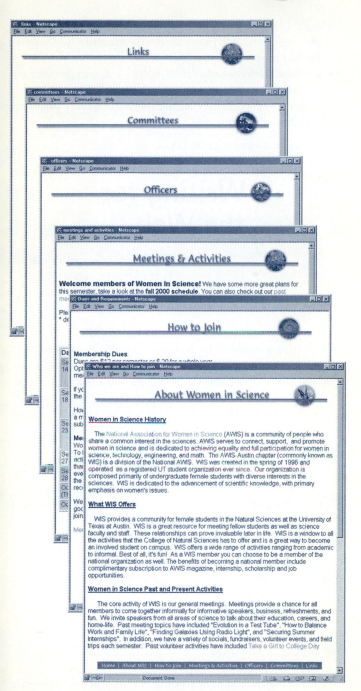

Figure 6.3 Content Pages

- the title is a clear description of your content; and for multiple-pages sites, each page includes the main title and subtitle for that page
- graphics reinforce rather than replace text, and graphics are as small as possible to avoid long download time
- links to other pages on your site are given on every page, and it is clear where links will take readers

7 Writing for the Web

"On the Internet, nobody knows you're a dog."
—PETER STEINER, cartoonist
(from a cartoon published in
The New Yorker)

Creating a World Wide Web site is similar in many respects to writing for print publication. You need to plan your work, based on your purpose and audience, and you need to write, revise, edit, and proofread your writing to be sure that it accomplishes what you want it to. Other aspects of producing a Web site are unique; we discuss them here.

EXPRESS!

Web documents use the HTML (HyperText Markup Language) electronic format. HTML tags tell Web browser programs how to display words and images and how to hyperlink separate documents to each other—the feature that makes the Web what it is.

To find examples of HTML coding, go to any Web location and from the "View" menu in your browser choose "Source" or "Page Source." You'll see a document containing the HTML codes for the page you were just viewing.

a Select a Method

Three basic methods of creating HTML documents require varying degrees of knowledge of HTML.

- *HTML text editors* require you to enter the HTML codes by hand. Although they don't have many user-friendly design tools, text editors are extremely flexible, since you can always compose with the latest Web standards and features.

- *Visual HTML editors* are also called "WYSIWYG" ("wizzy-wig") editors, which stands for "What You See Is What You Get." You don't need to know HTML because visual HTML design tools allow you to edit material as it would look in a Web browser. These tools don't always support the latest design features, however.

- "*Save as*" or *"Export" HTML options* in word processors and other kinds of software allow you to convert your work to HTML using your program's menu options. This method is fast and easy, but the generated pages often need fine-tuning to make them appealing.

Combine these methods to take advantage of the strengths each one offers. For example, you might start a page by quickly exporting an existing document to HTML, and afterward add features with a visual editor.

When you are writing a Web page, focus on your content in the first draft; don't start HTML coding until you have gone through at least one revision of your content. However, keep each page in a separate file right from the beginning. This will help you remember to craft each page as a separate entity capable of standing on its own. (Plan well: Put all your files for a project in the same directory; later, when you create links between the pages, you won't have to do as much typing.) You may want to start drafting your design at the same time as your content. However, if you are new to coding, keep your content and coding separate until you are sure your content is nearly final.

b Choose a Format

Decide early in your design process how you want to organize your Web page: Will you create a single, scrolling page or multiple pages connected by links? If you have a limited amount of information to present—as in a personal home page, résumé, or brief report—consider choosing a single, scrolling page. If you have more than two or three screens of information, however,

Figure 7.1 A Hierarchy

consider creating a set of pages connected by links. Most online readers don't like to scroll much beyond a few screens.

If you decide to create a multipage site, arrange your information so readers can navigate the pages easily. You'll need to create a home page as the entry into the site. Material deeper in the site may be connected to the home page in different ways, depending on your purpose and subject.

A hierarchy.   A hierarchy organizes pages into gradually more specific groupings. Readers find material by starting with general categories or topics and then working their way down to more specific information (Figure 7.1).

A sequence.   Sequential sites present readers with fewer options. Readers are encouraged to select "next page" rather than choose from a menu of options (Figure 7.2).

A hub.   A hub structure encourages exploration. The home page links to related pages that neither require a specific order of reading nor fit into clear hierarchies (Figure 7.3). Readers can browse each page, going back and forth from the home page.

As you build your site, keep these general suggestions in mind.

- Make sure all pages link to your home page.
- Don't create "dead ends" that require endless clicking on the "Back" button to find new content.

Figure 7.2 Sequential Organization

Figure 7.3 A Hub Structure

- Use hypertext links to cross-reference material you discuss on a number of pages.
- As your site grows, consider providing a "site map," a special page that outlines the organization of your material.
- When you link to Web pages outside of your site, make it clear to readers that they are being taken somewhere else.

c Gather Your Materials

Assemble whatever materials you want on your site in electronic formats that are accessible to those browsing the Web. For example, photographs need to be "digitized" by a scanner and converted to JPEG or GIF files (two graphics formats that are Web-compatible). To digitize photos, make animations, or record voices, you'll need to use specific software programs.

As you collect your materials, create a working folder on your disk and place all your materials in it. When you're ready to publish your project, you can simply upload the entire folder to the Web server (see page 43).

d Draft Your HTML Documents

The way you draft HTML documents will depend on which method of Web page composition you use. Keep in mind the differences between drafting home pages and content pages. Home pages have less rigid layout standards, since you will use that layout only once on your site. Content pages, however, should use a consistent format to present the site's most important material. See page 37 for an example.

During the planning and drafting stages, keep in mind the features that distinguish Web sites from printed sources.

- Visitors to Web sites are expecting a more graphical experience than they usually get from printed sources. When possible, use pictures, graphs, and animations to convey information.
- As its name indicates, the World Wide Web connects people and ideas across the globe. Take advantage of this interconnectedness by inserting links to other, related Web sites in your site.

- Because of the allure of the Web's vast offerings, visitors to your site may not linger very long. Therefore, be sure that your site is attractively designed and that important information is quickly accessible.

e Upload Your Page

As you work on your page, you can preview it on your browser, but to publish it on the Web, you'll need to upload it. If you are composing a project for class, your instructor will give you uploading instructions. If you are composing pages for yourself or your organization, you'll probably need to establish an account with an Internet service provider, which might be your college or university. In any case, prepare your files for uploading by making sure they follow Internet file name conventions.

- Don't use any spaces or punctuation in your file names, except a period before the final suffix. You can separate words with underscores ("_") instead of spaces.
- Use the appropriate file suffix: ".html" or ".htm" for HTML documents; ".jpg" or ".gif" for graphics; ".txt" for plain text.
- Use all lowercase letters (suggested so you will not have to remember later whether you used any capital letters in file names).

e-TIPS

For Web projects with external links, check the other sites you intend to link to and make sure they are still active before you code the links. Check all your links once more before you turn in your final project. Web sites shift around with amazing rapidity.

<DESTINATIONS>

For a guide to HTML tags, visit Kevin Werbach's *The Bare Bones Guide to HTML* at <http://werbach.com/barebones/barebones.html> or *A Beginner's Guide to HTML* at <http://www.ncsa.uiuc.edu/General/Internet/WWW/HTMLPrimer.html>.

For a beginner's guide to creating Web pages, visit "HTML for Beginners" at <http://www.cpcug.org/user/houser/>.

For detailed information on Web site and page design, visit the "Web Style Guide" at <http://www.webstyleguide.com/index.html?/contents.html>.

For an amusing discussion of bad Web design, visit *Web Pages that Suck* at <http://www.webpagesthatsuck.com>. ■

Related E-Tips

- Organizing informational Web sites: see pages 14–15
- Making storyboards for multipage sites: see page 15
- Drafting content and design separately: see page 39
- Using links as documentation: see page 43

Research

8 Finding Information

"If we knew what it is we were doing, it would not be called research, would it?"
—ALBERT EINSTEIN, scientist

Most college writing projects will require research both in the library and online. The sheer number of sources that seem to bear on your topic may be daunting; a wealth of material is available in print and online media. You can make sense of the riches if you are systematic and dogged in your efforts. Don't give up too soon when you can't immediately locate the materials you want. But don't be satisfied, either, if your initial searches produce more riches than you expect. Always push deeper into the archives, libraries, and networks.

EXPRESS!

Note cards are still a good tool for keeping track of bibliographical information. Each bibliography card should contain all the information you would need to find a source later, including the following.

- the author's last name and the title of the work
- the publisher, its location, and the publication date
- page numbers or URL for locating the source
- for electronic sources such as a Web site or newsgroup, the date you accessed the source
- for printed sources, a library call number or location

---

a Consult Library Sources

Your first priority is to become familiar with the libraries and research facilities on your campus. Begin exploring your research subject by examining the library's holdings.

Use library catalogs.   Most libraries provide access to their catalogs via computers. These electronic catalogs can be searched by author, title, subject, and keywords, and they will provide you with the titles and call numbers of books related to your search terms.

<DESTINATION>

Some library catalogs can be searched via the World Wide Web; some also allow you to request materials from your school library using interlibrary loan. For a list of online library catalogs, visit the *Libweb* index of "Library Servers via WWW" at <http://sunsite.berkeley.edu/libweb>. ■

Locate bibliographies.   Bibliographies are lists of books, articles, and other documentary materials that deal with particular subjects or subject areas. You will save time if you can locate an existing printed bibliography—preferably an annotated one—on your subject. Useful bibliographies include the following.

> *Bibliographies in American History*
> *Guide to the Literature of Art History*
> *A Guide to the Literature of Astronomy*
> *Science and Engineering Literature*
> *MLA International Bibliography*
> *Using the Mathematical Literature*
> *Music Reference and Research Materials*
> *Harvard List of Books in Psychology*

Consult indexes, abstracts, and databases.   Indexes—printed and electronic—list the journal articles, magazine pieces, and newspaper stories that cannot be recorded in a library catalog. Check your library's Web site to find out which databases and indexes your library subscribes to. All provide publication information; some also give abstracts of articles or the articles themselves. Others also offer full texts of news stories, literary works, historical documents, and so on. Multidisciplinary indexes include the following.

> *ArticleFirst* (OCLC) (electronic)
> *Expanded Academic ASAP* (electronic)
> *Academic Search Elite* (EBSCO) (electronic)
> *Readers' Guide Abstracts* (electronic)
> *Readers' Guide to Periodical Literature* (print)

Discipline-specific indexes, both print and electronic, include the following.

Anthropology   *Anthropological Literature*
Art   *Art Abstracts*

Business	*Business Periodicals Index; ABI Inform*
Chemistry	*CAS*
Current affairs	*Lexis-Nexis*
Education	*Education Index, ERIC*
Engineering	*INSPEC*
Film	*Film Index International; Art Index*
History	*Historical Abstracts; America: History and Life*
Humanities	*FRANCIS; Humanities Index*
Literature	*Essay and General Literature Index; MLA Bibliography*
Mathematics	*MathSciNet*
Philosophy	*Philosopher's Index*
Psychology	*Psychological Abstracts; PsycLit; PsycINFO*
Religion	*ATLA Religion Database*
Science	*General Science Index; General Science Abstracts*
Social Sciences	*Social Science & Humanities Index*

‹DESTINATIONS›

Two services that allow users to search large databases of journal articles are Northern Light ‹http://northernlight.com› and Ingenta ‹http://www.ingenta.com›. Downloading or printing a full-text article incurs a fee, but you can also use these services to locate relevant citations and then search for the printed articles in your college library. ■

Consult biographical resources.   For a good source of information about famous people, start with the *Biography Index: A Cumulative Index to Biographic Material in Books and Magazines, Bio-Base, Lexis-Nexis, Current Biography,* and *The McGraw-Hill Encyclopedia of World Biography.*

There are also various *Who's Who* volumes and dictionaries of biography. Three famous dictionaries of biography are the *Dictionary of National Biography* (British), the *Dictionary of American Biography,* and *Webster's New Biographical Dictionary.*

More narrowly focused biographical volumes include the following.

Dictionary of African Biography
Dictionary of American Negro Biography
Encyclopedia of Asian History
Australian Dictionary of Biography
Dictionary of Canadian Biography

Mexican American Biography
Index to Women

Locate statistics. Statistics about every imaginable topic are available in library reference rooms and online. Use up-to-date and reliable figures in your presentations. Sources include the following.

World Almanac (general)
Current Index to Statistics (general)
Statistical Abstract of the United States
STAT-USA (United States)
GPO Access (United States)
National Intelligence Factbook (world)
Handbook of Basic Economic Statistics
Survey of Current Business
Gallup Poll (public opinion)

‹DESTINATION›

For statistics from more than seventy agencies of the federal government, visit *FedStats* at ‹http://www.fedstats.gov›. ∎

Check news sources. The newspapers most widely available in American libraries are the *New York Times* and the *Wall Street Journal.* For information more than eight or nine years old, you'll need to use printed papers or microfilm copies.

For more recent events, try the following.

NewsBank, an electronic file of more than 400 American newspapers keyed to a microfiche collection
Facts on File, a weekly summary of national and international news
CQ Researcher, a source for background information on major problems and controversies
Editorials on File, a sampling of world and national opinion

‹DESTINATIONS›

For very current events, you can search the hundreds of newspapers and news services currently online, including the following.

C-SPAN Online   ‹http://www.c-span.org›
Fox News   ‹http://www.foxnews.com›

London Times	<http://www.the-times.co.uk/>
New York Times	<http://www.nytimes.com>
Reuters	<http://www.reuters.com/news/>
USA Today News	<http://www.usatoday.com> ■

Check book and film reviews.   To locate reviews of books, see *Book Review Digest, Book Review Index,* or *Current Book Review Citations.* For film reviews and criticism, see the printed volumes *Film Review Index* and *Film Criticism: An Index to Critics' Anthologies,* as well as the electronic *Film Index International.*

e-TIPS

It is important to know the difference between electronic sources accessed through databases such as those just listed and electronic information that comes directly from the Internet. Full-text articles that you access from a database such as Expanded Academic, for example, are duplicates of printed sources (and therefore they have gone through an editing/publishing process), or they come from well-established and respected electronic publications. Electronic material accessed through databases is, therefore, more reliable than what you might find when you surf the Internet using search engines. You can find good information this way, too, but you must be especially careful to evaluate what you find because anyone can publish anything on the Web.

b Search Online Sources

To supplement the information you find in printed works, use the Internet to locate helpful information and to discuss your topic with other researchers.

Check the World Wide Web.   The World Wide Web provides access to an enormous amount of information. However, the quality of information on the Web varies a great deal: Some reputable sites offer information that has been evaluated and edited, but others offer slanted views at best. Approach the Web with caution as a resource for research, recognizing the differences in purpose and quality among sites. You need all of your critical powers when surveying Web sites for information. (See pages 53–58 for more advice about evaluating sources.)

Web search engines are the best tools for finding information. Each one works a little differently from the others, and all have particular strengths and weaknesses. Research your subject area on more than one search engine to explore their holdings. The following are the best-known search engines.

AltaVista	<http://www.altavista.com>
Excite	<http://www.excite.com>
Google	<http://www.google.com>
HotBot	<http://www.hotbot.com>
Yahoo!	<http://www.yahoo.com>

For advice on evaluating Web search engines and tips on Web search techniques, visit *Search Engine Watch* at <http://searchenginewatch. internet.com>.

   Hundreds of reference sites have also been created by libraries, universities, and government institutions. Here are just a few places to look.

Argus Clearinghouse	<http://www.clearinghouse.net/>
Books on the Internet	<http://222.utexas.edu/books.etext.html>
English Server (CMU)	<http://eserver.org>
InfoSurf	<http://www.infosurf.com>
Internet Public Library	<http://ipl.org>
Knowledge Source (SIRS)	<http://knowledgesource.com>
The WWW Virtual Library	<http://vlib.org>

c Understand Keyword Searching

   A keyword search scans all the titles (and sometimes all the text) in a catalog, database, or on the Web containing the keyword(s) you have typed into a box or line on the screen.

   Some electronic search engines use Boolean searching, a technique that gives you more control over what you are searching. These are the standard commands.

AND   Using AND between keywords delivers sources containing all of the keywords you typed.

         Patrick AND O'Brian (delivers all sources containing both "Patrick" and "O'Brian")

OR   Using OR between keywords directs the search engine to
            find any examples of either keyword, allowing you to lo-
            cate all documents that cover related concepts.

            Congress OR Senate

NOT   Using NOT between terms permits you to specify sites
            with one term but not another, excluding certain mean-
            ings of a term that are irrelevant to your search.

            Orioles NOT Baltimore

( )   Putting parentheses around items allows for more fine-
            tuning. The following example locates documents that
            mention either Senator Gramm or Senator Hutchison
            but no other senators.

            Senator AND (Gramm OR Hutchison)

" "   Putting quotation marks around a phrase, such as "nov-
            els of Patrick O'Brian," brings up only items that con-
            tain the phrase in its entirety and narrows the list of
            items considerably.

Some search engines use plus (+) and minus (−) to direct some of
the same functions. Take a few minutes to read the "help" files for
indexes, catalogs, or Web search engines to discover the tools designed to maximize your search.

d | Conduct Field Research

Conducting field research of your own can provoke insights
you may not get from reading library and online sources—
especially if your topic has a local emphasis.

Interview experts.   An interview with an expert—face-to-face,
over the phone, or via email—adds credibility, authenticity, and
immediacy to a research project. For email interviews, contact the
expert and ask whether he or she is willing to help you with your
research before you send a lengthy list of questions. For face-to-
face or phone interviews, follow these guidelines.

- Request an interview in advance, and make it clear why you
  want the interview.
- Be on time for your appointment.
- Be prepared: Have a list of questions and follow-ups ready.
- Take careful notes, especially if you intend to quote the
  source.

- Double-check direct quotations, and be sure your source is willing to be quoted in your project.
- If you plan to tape the interview, get your subject's approval before turning the machine on.
- Promise to provide a copy of your completed paper.
- Send a note of thanks.

Write or email professional organizations.   Almost every subject, cause, concept, or idea is represented by a professional organization, society, bureau, office, or lobby. To look for Web sites or mailing addresses, consult the *Encyclopedia of Associations.*

‹DESTINATION›

The U.S. government offers a wealth of information. Start your search at ‹http://www.fedworld.gov›. ■

9   Evaluating Sources

> *"USA Today has come out with a new survey—apparently, three out of every four people make up 75 percent of the population."*
> —DAVID LETTERMAN, host of the *Late Show*

The value of a source depends on both its trustworthiness— "the quality of what you know"—and the way you intend to use it. For example, if you were writing a report on the official positions taken by the Democrats and Republicans in a long-past presidential election, you'd probably depend on scholarly books and articles, as well as newspaper accounts archived in the library. However, if you were writing about a current political campaign, you might read the views expressed in current campaign literature, recent magazines, and even Web sites and Usenet newsgroups. These sources might lack the authority and perspective of scholarly books or even official party materials, but they would still provide an excellent survey of political attitudes.

Even if sources can't be described as simply "good" or "bad" without considering their purposes, they do have strengths and weaknesses you must weigh when working on particular projects.

EXPRESS!

After you've decided a source is reliable and suited to the purpose of your research project, you should "position" it within your project. When you position a source, you identify its perspectives, biases, strengths, and limitations so that you do not misrepresent the information when you report it. Not all sources can be used in the same way. For example, some materials offer the most up-to-date and responsible treatment of a subject, while others have distinct points of view. Others might be "off the wall" but nonetheless make revealing points about culture and society. Positioning a source will help you stay conscious of the contexts that can shape and influence sources.

Positioning is more of a mental exercise than a written exercise. Still, the example below may help you think about what kinds of questions to ask about a source.

POSITIONING AN EDITORIAL TITLED "LEAVE THE PEOPLE HOME" BY ALEX ROLAND

"Leave the People Home" is an editorial that appeared in *USA Today* on July 7, 1997, following the successful landing on Mars of a research robot. The piece, written by Alex Roland, appears as a rebuttal to the paper's official editorial position endorsing exploration of Mars by human explorers. Owned by Gannett, *USA Today* is a daily newspaper available throughout the country with a predominantly liberal editorial page. It routinely publishes counterpoints to its editorials. *USA Today* notes that Alex Roland is "chair of the history department at Duke University, teaches technology history and is a former NASA historian." Roland's academic

credentials and work with the American space
agency would seem to give him authority on
this subject. The editorial was accessed
online on July 7, 2005, for a research project
examining how press coverage of the U.S. space
program has changed over the past ten years.

a Evaluate Print and Database Sources

These sources are generally reliable because they have been
screened by publishers and librarians. But this does not mean they
are always the best sources for your research project.

- Scholarly books and articles are among the most carefully
  researched, reviewed, and edited sources, although they are
  rarely current because it takes time to prepare and publish
  them. Their authors are recognized authorities, and their
  assertions are fully documented.
- Serious trade books and articles are written for well-educated
  but nonexpert readers who wish to acquire more than general knowledge about a subject. Serious periodicals include
  *Scientific American, New York Review of Books, The New Re-
  public, National Review,* and *Humanist.*
- Popular magazines and books (print or online) tend to be
  less demanding and shorter than serious or scholarly materials. Their sources may not be specifically identified, documented, or linked. Some familiar popular magazines include
  Time, Psychology Today, and *Smithsonian.*
- Newspapers and news organizations (print and online) provide up-to-date and generally reliable information about
  current events, as well as many features chronicling popular
  culture and political opinion. Published daily or weekly,
  newspapers lack the perspective of scholarly works but play
  an essential documentary function. Most news sources have
  political biases that you should take into account.

b Evaluate Internet Sources

New technologies mean that more and more sources come
to you directly from their authors, unreviewed and unrefereed by

publishers and librarians. Therefore, you must lean heavily on your critical skills to separate the good sources from the bad ones.

- Sponsored Web sites, created and supported by well-known institutions, organizations, and companies, share in the credibility of their supporting groups. Thus, Web sites posted by the U.S. government or by colleges and universities can usually be trusted.

- Online news organizations, such as *CNN Online* and *MSNBC*, provide up-to-date and generally reliable information about current events, popular culture, and political opinion.

- Individual Web sites are rarely refereed or reviewed by third parties who might take some responsibility for their accuracy. Confirm any hard facts in a second, more traditional source. When corresponding with an authority by email, be sure to record accurately both your questions and the expert's answers.

- Listservs and Usenet newsgroups can provide a way of learning quickly about current interests and debates related to your topic. As in any extended conversation, however, participants may vary widely in what they know; facts and figures may be reported unreliably; and the actual credibility of participants may be unknown.

e-TIPS

The domain of a Web site can help you to determine what kind of site it is and may, therefore, help you to determine how reliable it is as a source. Look at the last three letters of the URL.

.com designates commercial Web sites (**.net** falls into this category as well)

.org signifies that the site belongs to an organization, although it does not specify exactly what type of organization maintains the site

.edu indicates that the site is hosted by a recognized educational institution

.gov tells you that the site is an official U.S. government Web site

<DESTINATION>

About.com at <http://about.com> offers lists of reliable Web sites on a wide variety of topics; each site has been reviewed and screened by an expert in the subject. ∎

c | Question Every Source

Examine each of your sources from several angles, using these questions.

- *Is the source authoritative and reputable?* Reputable books, authors, reference tools, and Web sites will be cited by other reputable sources.
- *Is the source stable and up-to-date?* Generally, support your projects by the most current and reputable information in a field, but aim for a mix of sources—some classic works from the past as well as some current sources.
- *What are the biases of the source?* Almost all sources have political, social, or religious points of view that shape the information they contain and exclude. Sometimes these biases are apparent: The editorial page of the *New York Times* tends to be "liberal" in its politics, and that of the *Wall Street Journal* tends to be "conservative." It may be harder to detect the biases of other sources, but be assured they are there. Ask instructors or librarians to help you select sources containing a spectrum of opinions.
- *What commercial messages appear alongside the source?* It's easy to ignore printed ads in magazines, but Web sites are often so thick with ads that they can be difficult to use. Sponsored sites may also reflect the commercial connections of their owners, especially when news organizations are owned by larger companies with entertainment or other commercial interests. What appears—or doesn't appear—on a site may be determined by who is supporting the message. Be aware of such attempts to influence your judgment.
- *How well does the source present key information?* The design of a source is of greater concern with Web sites than with printed books and articles. A quality Web site does the following.

  - identifies its purpose clearly
  - arranges information logically
  - uses graphics to enhance its mission
  - furnishes relevant and selective links to other responsible resources
  - provides the identity and email address of the author/sponsor and the date of the posting

Remember to consult librarians and instructors. These people often have the expertise to cut a lengthy list of sources to the three or four you should not miss.

e-TIPS

The Web is full of outdated sites, posted and abandoned by their authors. To find the date of a Web site's original posting or its most recent update, check the bottom of the site's first page or the "About This Site" section.

<DESTINATION>

For a bibliography on evaluating information on the Internet, visit the *Information Quality WWW Virtual Library* at <http://www.vuw.ac.nz/~agsmith/evaln/evaln.htm>.

See also the Destination on page 56. ■

10   Using Sources

"It is curiosity, initiative, originality, and the ruthless application of honesty that count in research—much more than feats of logic and memory alone."
—JULIAN HUXLEY, biologist

As you gather research materials, read them critically in terms of your research question or tentative thesis. Does a source advance your argument, fill a hole in your background information, or perhaps change your opinion? Approach all sources actively and intensely, reading them slowly, and then thinking deeply about their implications and ideas. This critical reading might—perhaps *should*—lead you to refine your initial thinking and do even more reading and research.

A good way to begin mining a source for information is to annotate it. As you read and think, annotate your sources—make comments, ask questions, and react to ideas, either directly on a photocopy, printout, or electronic file, or by writing your responses in a notebook. Annotation helps you to identify ideas and information worth returning to and, more important, to engage in a dialogue with the authors and sources you encounter.

When you mark key passages—with a pen or the annotation feature on your word processor—be sure to add a note to yourself that explains the importance of the passage or states your reaction to it.

a   Academic Honesty

Unless you indicate otherwise, your reader will assume that the ideas and the language you use in your writing are your own. To uphold "academic honesty" you must be sure that your readers' assumptions are accurate. When you use language or ideas from another source, you must indicate this usage according to academic conventions.

It is not considered academically honest to improperly document sources simply because you do not understand how to paraphrase or cite your sources. It is your responsibility to master these skills and to apply them to all of your written work. This chapter will help you to do just that.

b   Paraphrase Accurately

A paraphrase usually reviews a complete source in some detail. When paraphrasing a work, you report its key information or restate its core arguments point by point in your own words. Follow these guidelines to prepare paraphrases.

- Put paraphrased material entirely in your own words, except for clearly marked quotations. Inadvertently copying the original author's words without quotation marks is plagiarism.
- Ensure that the paraphrase reflects the structure of the original piece and the ideas of the original author.

- Document each important fact or direct quotation with a specific page number from the source.
- Paraphrase only the material that is relevant to your research topic.

Reprinted following is "Gray Wolves Thrive in Montana After Decade" by Becky Bohrer, an article that appeared in the *Washington Post* on January 10, 2005. A paraphrase follows the article.

Gray Wolves Thrive in Montana After Decade
by Becky Bohrer

BILLINGS, Mont.—It was a frigid January day a decade ago when the first gray wolves bolted out of crates and into the wilds of Idaho. The event was cheered by environmentalists, who had once wondered if they would ever see wolves reintroduced into the Northern Rockies, and decried by ranchers and others who had hoped it would never happen.

Ten years later, passions still run deep. The wolves' incredible recovery and expansion in Montana, Idaho and Wyoming have ensured that.

Ranchers worry about livestock being attacked. Hunting organizers worry the wolves are decimating elk herds and threatening their livelihood.

Conservationists acknowledge problems but say wolves haven't been the scourge some predicted. They say wolves have helped the ecology of the greater Yellowstone area and economies of communities around Yellowstone National Park, where wolves also were reintroduced and are now a major attraction.

Some conservationists say the true measure of success will come when the wolves are taken off the list of animals protected by the Endangered Species Act, a move that, despite the wolves' having already achieved recovery goals, could be years away because of litigation.

"The book needs to be closed in order for us to say that the Endangered Species Act is doing its job and that wolf restoration is a complete success," said Jon Schwedler, a spokesman for the Predator Conservation Alliance in Bozeman, Mont.

Wolves in the region gained protection under the act in 1974, after being essentially wiped out in Idaho, Wyoming and Montana earlier in the century. But in the 1980s, a small number migrated naturally into Glacier National Park from Canada.

The U.S. Fish and Wildlife Service, in a 1987 plan, proposed reintroducing an "experimental" population in Yellowstone. After years of debate, the government decided in the early 1990s to reintroduce wolves to the park and parts of central Idaho.

Ranchers were firmly opposed, worried how the predators would affect their livelihoods.

"When they're killing a calf, they're not as warm and fuzzy as they're portrayed," said Jake Cummins, executive vice president of the Montana Farm Bureau Federation.

On Jan. 14, 1995, the first gray wolves were released in Idaho. Wolves bound for Yellowstone stayed in "acclimation pens" for two months before their release in March 1995, in hopes new packs would bond and the wolves would accept their surroundings as home turf.

The next year, 37 more wolves were reintroduced. Federal wildlife officials had expected to reintroduce animals for five years but stopped after two because the population was growing on its own.

Coexistence between ranchers and wolves has sometimes been uneasy. The Defenders of Wildlife pays compensation for confirmed losses and offers assistance with nonlethal measures to help keep wolves from livestock. But farm leaders say it's often difficult to prove losses and that little short of a shotgun will keep wolves from returning.

According to the government, 278 cattle and nearly 800 sheep were confirmed killed by wolves in the three states from 1995 to 2003. Meanwhile, 201 "problem" wolves also were killed, most by government agents.

Gray wolves reached recovery goals in 2002; an estimated 825 or more wolves live in Montana, Idaho and Wyoming. Before the government can propose that wolves in the Northern Rockies be delisted, each of the three states must have approved management plans.

The agency approved plans by Montana and Idaho last year, but rejected Wyoming's, which would have allowed wolves to be shot with little restriction in parts of that state. Wyoming is suing over the rejection.

With delisting delayed, the government has given Montana and Idaho more leeway in handling wolves in the interim. Ranchers there will be able to kill wolves without prior written approval if they can prove the animals are harassing livestock. Wolf kills still must be backed by physical evidence, such as bitten livestock or broken fences.

Looking back, those on all sides of the debate say emotions are still strong.

Maury Jones, an outfitter in western Wyoming, said he wishes reintroduction never happened, and swears it will be the "greatest wildlife disaster ever seen."

But Doug Smith, the Yellowstone wolf project leader, said the reintroduction has been a scientist's dream, providing an opportunity to compare an ecosystem with and without a key predator.

"It's one of the major conservation efforts of the 20th century, and to be there and watch the population grow and study it—it's one of the most exciting things that's happened to me," he said.

PARAPHRASE

In a 2005 *Washington Post* article, Becky Bohrer reports that once–endangered gray wolves are thriving in Montana, Idaho, and Wyoming a decade after the U.S. Fish and Wildlife Service reintroduced them to the area as part of a controversial conservation plan. When the wolves first qualified for protection under the Endangered Species Act in 1974, the species had been "virtually wiped out" in this country. The agency responded by releasing small groups of wolves into the area in 1995 and 1996. More than a decade later, the wolves are thriving and the population has grown to 825. Yet, according to Bohrer, controversy over the wolves' presence continues. Ranchers and hunters want fewer restrictions on dealing with wolves that kill livestock or other animals; many are lobbying to have the species removed from the endangered species list so that they can legally kill wolves who threaten their livelihood. Environmentalists, on the other hand, believe that the wolves are a vital part of the area's ecosystem and thus deserve protection. Although many would be happy to see the wolves achieve "non-endangered" status, they worry that without some legal protections in place, the successes of the repopulation program may be short-lived.

c Summarize Clearly

A summary captures the gist of a source or some portion of it, boiling it down to a few words or sentences. Summarize those materials that support your thesis but do not provide an extended argument or idea you need to share with readers.

When summarizing a source, identify the key facts or ideas and put them in your own words. In long sources, look for topic ideas in each major section. Then assemble these ideas into a short, coherent statement about the whole piece, only as detailed as you need for your project. For example, here is a summary of the source on pages 60–61.

SUMMARY

A recent news story by Becky Bohrer reports that gray wolves, once nearly extinct in this country, are now thriving in several northwestern states—thanks to an experimental repopulation program instituted by the U.S. Fish and Wildlife Service. Despite some conflicts among ranchers and environmentalists in the area over how the growing wolf population should be handled, the program has been so successful that the species may soon be removed from the endangered species list.

d | Use Direct Quotations Carefully

A direct quotation is any material repeated word for word from a source. Direct quotations in college papers always require some form of documentation. Similarly, identify the sources for any diagrams, statistics, charts, or pictures. For detailed discussions, with examples, of the major documentation styles such as MLA, see Chapters 11–14.

Select direct quotations strategically.   Every quotation in a piece of writing should contribute something your own words cannot convey. Use quotations for these purposes.

- to focus on a well-stated key idea in a source
- to show what others think about a subject—experts or the general public
- to lend support to facts or concepts
- to add strength or character to your argument or report
- to clarify or emphasize a point

Introduce all direct and indirect quotations.   Use a context or frame to introduce all borrowed material. Such frames can precede, follow, or interrupt the borrowed words or ideas. Adjust the frame to fit grammatically with the quotation, or, if necessary, select the quotation to fit the sentence.

FRAME PRECEDES BORROWED MATERIAL

In 1896, Woodrow Wilson, who would become Princeton's president in 1902, declared, "It is not learning but the spirit of service that will give a college a place in the public annals of the nation."   —Ernest L. Boyer

FRAME FOLLOWS BORROWED MATERIAL

"One reason you may have more colds if you hold back tears is that, when you're under stress, your body puts out steroids which affect your immune system and reduce your resistance to disease," **Dr. Broomfield comments.**
                    —Barbara Lang Stern

FRAME INTERRUPTS BORROWED MATERIAL

"Whatever happens," he [Karl Marx] **wrote grimly to Engels,** "I hope the bourgeoisie as long as they exist will have cause to remember my carbuncles."   —Paul Johnson

\<DESTINATION\>

For 150 verbs you can use in place of the verb *said* when quoting someone, visit Weber State University's Writing Center at \<http://departments.weber.edu/writingcenter/Handouts.htm\>. ■

Use ellipses (...) to show omissions.   Only part of a long quotation may suit your essay; ellipses allow you to present only the appropriate portion. Ellipses show where you have omitted material. If you use ellipses, be sure the omission doesn't change the meaning of the original passage.

> Although working with any part of an original scripture text is difficult, Barry Hoberman, author of "Translating the Bible," describes the text of the Old Testament as **"the stuff of scholarly nightmares."** He explains that while **"the entire New Testament was written within fifty to a hundred years, the books of the Old Testament were composed and edited over a period of about a thousand. . . . The oldest portions of the Old Testament . . . are probably a group of poems that appear . . . to date from roughly the twelfth and eleventh centuries B.C."**

Use [*sic*] to indicate an obvious error.   To show that you have copied a passage accurately—errors and all—place the expression *sic* in brackets one space after any mistake.

> Mr. Vincent's letter went on: "I would have preferred a younger bride, but I decided to marry the old window [*sic*] anyway."

Place short prose quotations between quotation marks. Longer quotations should be indented. For guidelines by documentation style, see pages 73 (MLA) and 113 (APA).

\<DESTINATION\>

For help with using quotations in MLA style, consult Purdue's Online Writing Lab at \<http://owl.english.purdue.edu/handouts/research/r_mla.html#Handling\>. ■

e Document Sources Precisely

Documentation is the evidence you provide to support the ideas presented in a research project. Some writers do not realize that by documenting sources inadequately or carelessly, they can destroy the credibility of their research.

Representing the words or ideas you found in a source as your own constitutes plagiarism, a serious charge against any writer. Quite simply, you should respect and acknowledge the work you borrow from other writers or colleagues.

Chapters 11–14 present four systems for documenting sources: Modern Language Association (MLA), American Psychological Association (APA), Chicago Manual of Style (CMS), and Council of Science Editors (CSE/CBE). Choose the style appropriate for your audience. Here we offer general guidelines for acknowledging and using sources.

Document information from sources fully.   Document all ideas, opinions, facts, and information that you acquire from sources and that cannot be considered common knowledge. Common knowledge includes the facts, dates, events, information, and concepts that can be looked up quickly in a standard reference book such as a dictionary or an encyclopedia.

For example, you can learn from an encyclopedia that the Battle of Waterloo was fought on June 18, 1815; thus, you do not have to document it. You also need not document common knowledge within a field—what's generally agreed on by experts. But if your subject is controversial, you may want to document even facts or ideas considered common knowledge. Consider your audience: Nonspecialist readers may need more documentation than experts in your research area.

Provide dates for important events, major figures, and works of literature and art. Identify any people readers might not recognize.

> After the great fire of London (1666), the city was . . .
>
> Henry Highland Garnet (1815–82), American abolitionist and radical, . . .

Acknowledge all direct and indirect uses of anyone else's work.   If you decide to quote all or part of a selection, you must use quotation marks or indentation to indicate that you are borrowing the writer's exact words. In academic papers, you must also identify the author, work, publisher, date, and location of the passage through formal documentation, such as MLA or APA.

If you quote a source indirectly, borrowing the information but not the words, you must include a parenthetical note acknowledging the source of the information. For example, if you paraphrase or summarize a source, you must document this indirect borrowing. For MLA examples, see pages 71–73. For APA, see pages 111–113.

e-TIPS

It is dangerously easy to plagiarize electronic sources inadvertently. Once a sentence or paragraph is in your file, it is extremely difficult to separate it from your own words. If you cut and paste a paragraph—even a sentence—be sure to document the source immediately in your notes.

Avoid plagiarism.   A proper summary or paraphrase of a source should be entirely in your own words. Some writers mistakenly believe that they can avoid a charge of plagiarism by rearranging or changing a few words in a selection; they are wrong.

Compare the plagiarized paraphrase and summary below with the acceptable versions on pages 62 and 63–64.

PLAGIARIZED PARAPHRASE

In a 2005 news article, Becky Bohrer reports that once–endangered gray wolves are thriving in the Northern Rockies a decade after the U.S. Fish and Wildlife Service reintroduced them to the area as part of a controversial conservation plan. The wolves' incredible recovery and expansion in Montana, Idaho, and Wyoming have come as a surprise to many. The species had been essentially wiped out in the region before it gained protection under the Endangered Species Act in 1974. Then the government decided in the early 1990s to release an experimental population of wolves into Yellowstone National Park and parts of Idaho. More than a decade later, the wolves are thriving and the population has grown—and so has the controversy. Ranchers worry about their livestock being attacked and hunters say the wolves are decimating the elk herds in the area. Environmentalists acknowledge the problems but say that wolves haven't been as harmful as some people predicted. Ranchers and hunters believe the wolves should be removed from the endangered species list and want more leeway in dealing with the wolves in the interim. Environmentalists want strong protections kept in place, since the program is one of the major conservation successes of the 20th century.

PLAGIARIZED SUMMARY

A recent news story reports that gray wolves, once essentially wiped out in this country, have seen an incredible recovery and expansion in Montana, Idaho, and Wyoming—thanks to a government–sponsored repopulation program. However, passions over the wolves' presence in the area still run deep. Ranchers and hunters worry the wolves are threatening their livelihood, while environmentalists say that wolves haven't been the scourge some predicted. The litigation and debate over how to manage the wolves could continue for years.

You'll see the faults very readily when you compare these plagiarized paragraphs with the opening paragraphs in Bohrer's original article on pages 60–61.

You can appreciate how tempting it might be to slip these words into the body of a paper, forgetting that you didn't write them yourself. To avoid plagiarism, the safest practice is to *always* use your own words in paraphrases and summaries.

e-TIPS

Links in hypertexts (such as World Wide Web pages) can function as a type of documentation: They can take readers directly to supporting material or sources. Use links judiciously—avoid too many on a page, and explain to your readers where a highlighted passage is leading them.

<DESTINATION>

For a comprehensive discussion about and examples of plagiarism, visit Student Judicial Services at the University of Texas at Austin at <http://deanofstudents.utexas.edu/sjs/academicintegrity.html>. ■

Documentation

11 MLA Style

"Life itself is a quotation."
—JORGE LUIS BORGES, writer, poet

The Modern Language Association (MLA) style of documentation is used in many professional fields in the humanities. The basic procedures for using MLA style are spelled out in this chapter. For any problems not addressed here, consult the *MLA Handbook for Writers of Research Papers,* seventh edition (2009). Style updates are also available at the MLA Web site at <http://www.mla.org>.

EXPRESS!

You need to take only two steps to use MLA style properly.

1. Create an in-text note for every source as you use it in a writing project.
2. Create an entry on a Works Cited page for each source you use.

Notice in the following example how the in-text note in parentheses tells readers to look for a work by Carter on the Works Cited page; they will find the quoted sentence on page 287 of Carter's book.

```
Many find modern society hectic and overpow-
ering: "we seem to spend all of our time
searching for bits of peace and quiet for
ourselves" (Carter 287).
```

Your readers can then turn to the Works Cited page for complete publication information about the source.

```
                    Works Cited
Carter, Stephen L. Civility: Manners, Morals,
    and the Etiquette of Democracy. New
    York: HarperPerennial, 1998. Print.
```

a | In-Text Citations

The main purpose of the in-text citation is to direct your reader to the original source of the information you are citing. See Section 11c, MLA Models, for more than sixty examples of in-text notes and their corresponding Works Cited entries. For formatting of in-text notes, see "In-Text Citations: MLA Format," page 73.

1. **A work that includes an author and page number**

   Either enclose the author's last name and the relevant page number(s) within parentheses, or name the author of the source in the body of the text and place only the page number within the parentheses.

   ```
   Many find modern society hectic and overpow-
   ering: "we seem to spend all of our time
   searching for bits of peace and quiet for
   ourselves" (Carter 287).
   ```

   ```
   Stephen L. Carter, professor of law at Yale,
   notes that "we seem to spend all of our time
   searching for bits of peace and quiet for
   ourselves" (287).
   ```

2. **A work without conventional authors or page numbers**

   Ordinarily, cite the source just by naming it or describing it within the body of the writing project itself.

   ```
   The Media Research Center Web site offers . . .
   ```

   ```
   The Arkansas State Highway Map indicates . . .
   ```

   ```
   Software such as Microsoft's FoxPro . . .
   ```

   If an electronic source includes paragraph numbers, screen numbers, or titles for the Web pages you are citing, you can put this helpful information in parentheses.

3. **A work without an author (but with page numbers)—for example, an unsigned article in a magazine or newspaper**

   List the title, shortened if necessary, and the page number. Shortened titles must always begin with the words used to alphabetize the entry on the Works Cited page.

("In the Thicket" 18)

Works Cited

"In the Thicket of Things." *Texas Monthly*
        Apr. 1994: 18. Print.

4. **More than one work by a single author**

Place a comma after the author's last name and identify the particular work being cited, using a shortened title.

(Altick, *Victorian People* 190-192)

(Altick, *Victorian Studies* 59)

Works Cited

Altick, Richard D. *Victorian People and*
        Ideas. New York: Norton, 1973. Print.
---. *Victorian Studies in Scarlet*. New York:
        Norton, 1977. Print.

5. **More than a single work in one note**

Separate the citations with a semicolon.

(Polukord 13-16; Ryan and Weber 126)

6. **Two or more sources in a single sentence**

Place the parenthetical notes right after the specific statements they support.

While the budget cuts might go deeper than
originally reported (Kinsley 42), there is no
reason to believe that "throwing more taxpayers' dollars into a bottomless pit" (Doggett
62) will do much to reform "one of the least
productive job training programs ever devised
by the federal government" (Will 28).

Notice that all the parenthetical notes are placed *outside* the quotation marks.

7. **Author quoted by another source**

Include "qtd. in" ("quoted in") before the name of the source.

(qtd. in Cavin 195)

8. **Quotations of more than four typed lines**

Indent a long quotation ten spaces from the left margin, omit quotation marks, and place the parenthetical note outside the final punctuation mark.

```
Winner of the Nobel Peace Prize in 1950,

Ralph Bunche, who died in 1971, left an en-

during legacy:

                    His memory lives on, especially

                    in the long struggle for human

                    dignity and against racial

                    discrimination and bigotry, and

                    in the growing effectiveness of

                    the United Nations in resolving

                    conflicts and keeping the peace.

                    (Urquhart 458)
```

In-Text Citations: MLA Format

- A single typed space separates the author's name and the page number: (Carter 287)
- The note itself falls *outside* the quotation marks: ". . . ourselves" (Carter 287)
- The final punctuation for the sentence comes *after* the note: (Carter 287).*
- Page numbers are not preceded by *p.* or *pp.* or by a comma: (Bly 253-54)

*Exception: The one exception is a quotation longer than four typed lines. See #8, above.

---

b The Works Cited Page

On a separate page at the end of your project, list alphabetically every source you cited. Include only sources you actually mention in the body of the project, not all that you might have examined in preparing the work. Title the list "Works Cited."

Works Cited Page: MLA Style

- Center the title "Works Cited" at the top of the page, with no quotation marks.
- Arrange the items alphabetically by the last name of the author. If no author is given, list the work according to the first word of its title, excluding *The, A,* and *An.*
- The first line of each entry touches the left-hand margin. Subsequent lines of an entry are indented five spaces.
- Double-space the entire list. Do not quadruple-space between entries unless your instructor asks you to.
- Punctuate items carefully. Don't forget the period at the end of each entry.
- If you have two or more entries by the same author, use the author's name for the first entry only. For subsequent entries, use three hyphens followed by a period. List the titles in alphabetical order. For an example, see #4, page 72.
- Shorten publishers' names whenever possible. Drop words such as *Company, Inc., LTD, Bro.,* and *Books.* Abbreviate *University* to *U* and *University Press* to *UP*. See also #21 on page 81.
- Always include the medium of publication (i.e., Print, Web, CD, etc.).

Works Cited

Arni, Sherry. "I Can Live with It." *English Journal* 79 (Nov. 1990): 76. Print.

"Chapters 110 and 128, Subchapter C." *Texas Education Agency Administrative Rules*. Texas Education Agency. 1 Sept. 1998. Web. 6 March 2000.

Corbett, H. Dickson, and Bruce L. Wilson. *Testing, Reform, and Rebellion*. Norwood: Ablex, 1991. Print.

---

c MLA Models

Following you will find MLA models to follow in creating in-text notes and the corresponding Works Cited entries for more than sixty kinds of sources. Simply locate the type of source you need to cite in the MLA Models Index and then locate that item by number in the list that follows.

MLA Models Index

(*continued*)

48. CD-ROM/diskette database or publication	56. Personal interview
49. Full-text database article	57. Musical composition
	58. Recording/audio clip
MISCELLANEOUS ENTRIES	59. Speech
50. Microfilm or microfiche	60. Lecture
51. Biblical citation	61. Advertisement
52. Videotape/DVD	62. Letter—published
53. Movie	63. Letter—unpublished
54. Television program	64. Artwork/photograph
55. Radio program	65. Drama or play

1. **Book, Generic—MLA** Provide author, title, place of publication, publisher, and year of publication.

   Note: (Prosek 246-47)

                   Works Cited
   Prosek, James. *The Complete Angler: A*
           Connecticut Yankee Follows in the
           Footsteps of Walton. New York:
           HarperCollins, 1999. Print.

2. **Book, Two or Three Authors or Editors—MLA**

   Note: (Collier and Horowitz 24)

                   Works Cited
   Collier, Peter, and David Horowitz.
           Destructive Generation: Second Thoughts
           About the '60s. New York: Summit, 1989.
           Print.

3. **Book, Four or More Authors or Editors—MLA** You have two options. You can name all the authors in both the parenthetical note and Works Cited entry.

   Note: (Guth, Rico, Ruszkiewicz, and
   Bridges 95)

                   Works Cited
   Guth, Hans P., Gabriele L. Rico, John
           Ruszkiewicz, and Bill Bridges. *The*
           Rhetoric of Laughter: The Best and Worst

> *of Humor Night*. Fort Worth: Harcourt,
> 1996. Print.

Alternatively, you can name just the first author given on the title page and use the Latin abbreviation *et al.,* which means "and others."

Note: (Guth et al. 95)

Works Cited

Guth, Hans P., et al. *The Rhetoric of
        Laughter: The Best and Worst of Humor
        Night*. Fort Worth: Harcourt, 1996. Print.

4. **Book, Revised by a Second Author—MLA**   Sometimes you may need to cite a book by its original author, even when it has been revised. In such a case, place the editor's name after the title of the book.

Note: (Guerber 20)

Works Cited

Guerber, Hélène Adeline. T*he Myths of Greece
        and Rome*. Ed. Dorothy Margaret Stuart.
        3rd ed. London: Harrap, 1965. Print.

5. **Book, Edited—Focus on the Original Author—MLA**

Note: (*Cor.* 3.3.119-35)

Works Cited

Shakespeare, William. *The Tragedy of
        Coriolanus*. Ed. Reuben Brower. New York:
        Signet, 1966. Print.

Coriolanus is a play by Shakespeare, so the note provides act, scene, and line numbers—not author and page numbers.

6. **Book, Edited—Focus on the Editor—MLA**

Note: (Brower xxiii-1)

Works Cited

Brower, Reuben, ed. *The Tragedy of
        Coriolanus*. By William Shakespeare. New
        York: Signet, 1966. Print.

7. **Book, Edited—Focus on the Editor, More Than One Editor—MLA**

   Note: (Kittredge and Smith xvi-xvii)

   Works Cited

   Kittredge, William, and Annick Smith, eds. *The Last Best Place: A Montana Anthology.* Seattle: U of Washington P, 1988. Print.

8. **Book, Written by a Group—MLA**

   Note: The Reader's Digest *Fix-It-Yourself Manual* explains the importance of a UL label (123).

   Works Cited

   Reader's Digest. *Fix-It-Yourself Manual.* Pleasantville: Reader's Digest, 1977. Print.

9. **Book with No Author—MLA**   List the book by its title ignoring *The, A,* or *An.*

   Note: (*Kodak* 56-58)
   Note: *The Kodak Guide to 35mm Photography* lists color film types in a useful chart (56-58).

   Works Cited

   The Kodak Guide to 35mm Photography. 6th ed. Rochester: Eastman, 1989. Print.

10. **Book, Focus on a Foreword, Introduction, Preface, or Afterword—MLA**

    Note: (O'Rourke 5)

    Works Cited

    O'Rourke, P. J. Introduction. *Road Trips, Head Trips, and Other Car-Crazed Writings.* Ed. Jean Lindamood. New York: Atlantic, 1996. 1-8. Print.

11. **Work of More Than One Volume—MLA**   When you use only one volume of a multivolume set, identify both the

volume you have used and the total number of volumes in the set.

Note: (Spindler 17-18)

Works Cited

Spindler, Karlheinz. *Abstract Algebra with Applications*. Vol. 1. New York: Dekker, 1994. 2 vols. Print.

If you use more than one volume of a set, identify the specific volumes in the parenthetical notes as you cite them. Then, in the Works Cited entry, list the total number of volumes in that set.

Notes: (Spindler 1: 17-18); (Spindler 2: 369)

Works Cited

Spindler, Karlheinz. *Abstract Algebra with Applications*. 2 vols. New York: Dekker, 1994. Print.

12. **Book, Translation—Focus on the Original Author—MLA**

Note: (Freire 137-38)

Works Cited

Freire, Paulo. *Learning to Question: A Pedagogy of Liberation*. Trans. Tony Coates. New York: Continuum, 1989. Print.

13. **Book, Translation—Focus on the Translator—MLA**

Note: (Swanton 17-18)

Works Cited

Swanton, Michael, trans. *Beowulf*. New York: Barnes, 1978. Print.

14. **Book in a Foreign Language—MLA**

Note: (Bablet and Jacquot 59)

Works Cited

Bablet, Denis, and Jean Jacquot. *Les Voies de la création théâtrale*. Paris: Editions

```
du Centre National de la Recherche
Scientifique, 1977. Print.
```

15. **Book, Republished—MLA**   Give original publication dates for works of fiction that have been through many editions and reprints.

    Note: (Herbert 146)

    Works Cited

    ```
    Herbert, Frank. Dune. 1965. New York:
        Berkeley, 1977. Print.
    ```

16. **Book, Part of a Series—MLA**   Give the series name just before the place of publication.

    Note: (Pemberton xii)

    Works Cited

    ```
    Pemberton, Michael, ed. The Ethics of Writing
        Instruction: Issues in Theory and
        Practice. Perspectives on Writing:
        Theory, Research, Practice 4. Stamford:
        Ablex, 2000. Print.
    ```

17. **Book, a Reader or Anthology—MLA**   When you quote from the front matter of the collection, the page numbers may sometimes be Roman numerals. (To cite a selection from within an anthology, see model #29 on page 84.)

    Note: (Lunsford and Ruszkiewicz xxi-xxvi)

    Works Cited

    ```
    Lunsford, Andrea A., and John J. Ruszkiewicz,
        eds. The Presence of Others: Voices and
        Images That Call for Response. 4th ed.
        New York: Bedford, 2003. Print.
    ```

18. **Book, a Second, Third, or Later Edition—MLA**

    Note: (Rombauer 480-81)

    Works Cited

    ```
    Rombauer, Marjorie Dick. Legal Problem
        Solving: Analysis, Research, and Writing.
        5th ed. St. Paul: West, 1991. Print.
    ```

19. Chapter in a Book—MLA

Note: (Shalit 144-60)

Works Cited

Shalit, Wendy. "Male Character." *A Return to Modesty: Discovering the Lost Virtue.* New York: Free, 1999. 144-60. Print.

20. Book Published Before 1900—MLA Omit the name of the publisher in citations to works published prior to 1900.

Note: (Bowdler 2: 47)

Works Cited

Bowdler, Thomas, ed. *The Family Shakespeare.* 10 vols. London, 1818. Print.

21. Book Issued by a Division of a Publisher—a Special Imprint—MLA Attach the special imprint (Vintage in this case) to the publisher's name with a hyphen.

Note: (Hofstader 192-93)

Works Cited

Hofstader, Douglas. *Gödel, Escher, Bach: An Eternal Golden Braid.* New York: Vintage-Random, 1980. Print.

22. Dissertation or Thesis—Published—MLA If published by University Microfilms International (UMI), provide the order number.

Note: (Rifkin 234)

Works Cited

Rifkin, Myra Lee. *Burial, Funeral and Mourning Customs in England, 1558-1662.* Diss. Bryn Mawr, 1977. Ann Arbor: UMI, 1977. DDJ78-01385. Microfilm.

23. Dissertation or Thesis—Unpublished—MLA The title appears between quotation marks.

Note: (Altman 150)

Works Cited

Altman, Jack, Jr. "The Politics of Health Planning and Regulation." Diss.

Massachusetts Institute of Technology,
1983. Print.

24. **Book Review/Movie Review—Titled or Untitled—MLA**
Not all reviews have titles, so the form for a review may vary
slightly.

Note: (Keen 39)

Works Cited

Keen, Maurice. "The Knight of Knights." Rev.
of *William Marshall: The Flower of
Chivalry*, by Georges Duby. *New York
Review of Books* 16 Jan. 1986: 39-40.
Print.

Notice that a book title (*Uncle Tom's Cabin*) within a book
title is not italicized (Uncle Tom's Cabin *and American
Culture*).

Note: (Baym 691-92)

Works Cited

Baym, Nina. Rev. of Uncle Tom's Cabin *and
American Culture*, by Thomas F. Gossett.
Journal of American History 72.1 (1985):
691-92. Print.

Here's the form for a film review found online—in this case,
in the e-zine *Slate*. The citation includes the date of the review itself and the date it was accessed online.

Note: David Edelstein finds Ben Affleck an
unlikely convict in *Reindeer Games* . . .

Works Cited

Edelstein, David. "Parlor Games." Rev. of
Reindeer Games, dir. John Frankenheimer.
Slate.com 25 Feb. 2000. Web. 8 Mar 2000.

25. **Article in a Scholarly Journal—MLA**   Scholarly journals are
usually identified by volume number or season. Such journals
may be paginated year by year, with a year's work treated as
one volume, or issue by issue. In either case, provide author,
title of article, title of journal, volume number, issue number,
date of publication, and page numbers.

Note: (Smith 301)

Works Cited

Smith, Laurajane. "Heritage Management as
     Postprocessual Archaeology?" *Antiquity*
     64.2 (June 1994): 300–09. Print.

Note: (Morgenroth 91–92)

Works Cited

Morgenroth, Joyce. "Dressing for the Dance"
     Wilson Quarterly 22.2 (Spring 1998):
     88–95. Print.

26. **Article in a Popular Magazine—MLA**   Magazines are paginated issue by issue and identified by the seasonal, monthly, or weekly date of publication. Provide author, title of article, title of magazine, date of publication, and page numbers.

Note: (Murray 63)

Works Cited

Murray, Spencer. "Roaming Wyoming." *Open Road*
     Spring 1999: 60–65. Print.

Articles in magazines often don't appear on consecutive pages. When that's the case, list the relevant page number(s) in the parenthetical note. In the Works Cited entry give the first page on which it appears, followed by a plus sign—for example, *112+*.

Note: (Mackay 170)

Works Cited

Mackay, Jordan. "A Murder on Campus." *Texas*
     Monthly Jan. 2000: 112+. Print.

27. **Article in a Weekly or Biweekly Magazine—MLA**

Note: (Smolowe 20)

Works Cited

Smolowe, Jill. "When Violence Hits Home."
     Time 18 July 1994: 18–25. Print.

28. **Article in a Monthly Magazine—MLA**

    Note: (Bond 90)

    Works Cited

    Bond, Constance. "If You Can't Bear to Part
        with It, Open a New Museum." *Smithsonian*
        Apr. 1995: 90-97. Print.

29. **Article or Selection from a Reader or Anthology—MLA**
    List the item on the Works Cited page by the author of
    the piece you are actually citing, not the editor(s) of the
    collection.

    Note: (King 417-20)

    Works Cited

    King, Robert. "Should English Be the Law?"
        *The Presence of Others: Voices and
        Images That Call for Response*. 3rd ed.
        Ed. Andrea Lunsford and John
        Ruszkiewicz. New York: Bedford, 2000.
        409-21. Print.

    When you cite two or more selections from a reader or an
    anthology, list that collection fully on the Works Cited page.

    Lunsford, Andrea, and John Ruszkiewicz, eds.
        *The Presence of Others: Voices and
        Images That Call for Response*. 4th ed.
        New York: Bedford, 2003. Print.

    Then, still in the Works Cited list, identify the authors and
    titles of all articles you cite from that reader or anthology,
    followed by the name of the editors and page numbers of
    those selections.

    Note: (King 417-20)
    Note: (Turkle 453)

    Works Cited

    King, Robert. "Should English Be the Law?"
        Lunsford and Ruszkiewicz 409-21. Print.
    Turkle, Shirley. "Who Am We?" Lunsford and
        Ruszkiewicz 442-58. Print.

30. **Article in a Newspaper—MLA** The plus sign indicates that an article continues beyond the designated page, but not necessarily on consecutive pages.

    Note: (Peterson 2A)

    Works Cited

    Peterson, Karen S. "Turns Out We Are
      'Sexually Conventional.'" *USA Today*
      7 Oct. 1994: 1A+. Print.

31. **Editorial in a Newspaper—Author Not Named—MLA**

    Note: ("Negro College" 28)

    Works Cited

    "Negro College Fund: Mission Is Still
      Important on 50th Anniversary."
      Editorial. *Dallas Morning News* 8 Oct.
      1994: A28. Print.

32. **Letter to the Editor—MLA**

    Note: (Cantu 4)

    Works Cited

    Cantu, Tony. Letter. *San Antonio Light*
      14 Jan. 1986, southwest ed.: C4. Print.

33. **Cartoon—MLA** Describe a cartoon in the text of your essay.

    Note: In the cartoon "Squib" by Miles
    Mathis . . .

    Works Cited

    Mathis, Miles. "Squib." Cartoon. *Daily Texan*
      15 Jan. 1986: 19. Print.

34. **Reference Work or Encyclopedia (Familiar or Online)—MLA** Identify the edition you are using by its date. Omit the names of editors and most publishing information. No page number is given in the parenthetical note when a work is arranged alphabetically.

    Note: (Benedict)

Works Cited

```
Benedict, Roger William. "Northwest Passage."
     Encyclopaedia Britannica: Macropaedia.
     1974 ed. Print.
```

A citation for an online encyclopedia article would include a date of access and electronic address. However, the online version might not list an author.

Works Cited

```
"Northwest Passage." Britannica Online.
     Encyclopaedia Britannica. Web. 8 Feb.
     2000.
```

35. **Reference Work (Specialized or Less Familiar)—MLA** With less familiar reference tools, a full entry is required. (See #34 above for a comparison with familiar reference works.)

Note: (Kovesi)

Works Cited

```
Kovesi, Julius. "Hungarian Philosophy." The
     Encyclopedia of Philosophy. Ed. Paul
     Edwards. 8 vols. New York: Macmillan,
     1967. Print.
```

36. **Bulletin or Pamphlet—MLA**

Note: (Morgan 8-9)

Works Cited

```
Morgan, Martha G., ed. Campus Guide to
     Computer & Web Services. Austin: U of
     Texas, 1999. Print.
```

37. **Government Document—MLA** Give the name of the government (national, state, or local) and the agency issuing the report, the title of the document, and publishing information. If it is a congressional document other than the *Congressional Record,* identify the Congress and, when important, the session (for example, *99th Cong., 1st sess.*) after the title of the document.

Note: This information is from the 1985-86 Official Congressional Directory (182-84).

```
                Works Cited
United States. Cong. Joint Committee on
        Printing. 1985-86 Official Congressional
        Directory. 99th Cong., 1st sess.
        Washington: GPO, 1985. Print.
```

To cite the *Congressional Record,* give only the date and page
number.

```
Cong. Rec. 8 Feb. 2003: 3942-43.
```

38. **Computer Software—MLA**   Give the author if known,
the version number if any (for example: *Microsoft
Word.* Vers. 7.0), the manufacturer, the date, and (option-
ally) the system needed to run it. Name the software in
your text.

Note: With software such as Connectix's
Virtual PC . . .

```
                Works Cited
Virtual PC. Vers. 3.0. San Mateo: Connectix,
        1999. Software.
```

39. **WWW Page—Generic—MLA**   A typical MLA Works
Cited entry for an electronic source may include the following information:

- Name of the creator, author, or compiler of the site, if any.
- Title of the work, in italics, unless it is part of a larger title,
  in which case enclose it in quotation marks.
- Title of the overall Web site, in italics, if this is distinct
  from the title of the work.
- Version or edition of the site, if relevant.
- Publisher or sponsor of the site. This information can
  often be found at the bottom of the Web page. If this in-
  formation is not available, use *n.p.* (for *no publisher*).
- Date of publication (day, month, year, if available). If no
  date is given, use *n.d.*
- Medium of publication. For all online sources, the
  medium of publication is *Web*.
- Date of access (day, month, year).

Usually you do not include URLs in works-cited entries.
However, if you think that your readers will not be able to

locate the source without this information, include the URL in your citation. If you do include a URL, format as follows:

- Place the URL as the last item in the entry, following the date of access, a period, and a space.
- Enclose the URL in angle brackets (<>) followed by a period.
- Give the complete URL, including the access-mode identifier (*http*, *ftp*, etc.). You may want to use your browser's copy-and-paste function to move the URL directly to your text.
- Break a URL only *after* a slash.
- Do not hyphenate a URL, and do not allow your software to insert a hyphen.

```
                    Works Cited
FindaPark.nps.gov. National Park Service.
      Web. 29 April 2009.
"African Burial Ground." FindaPark.nps.gov.
      National Park Service. Web. 29 April
      2009.
```

e-TIPS

Since most Web sites and other online sources do not have page numbers, avoid in-text parenthetical citations by identifying the site in the body of the paper.

40. WWW—Online Book—MLA For online sources also available in print, use the format for print sources and include the title of the database or Web site, the medium of publication (Web), and the date of access.

Note: In the online version of Henry Adams's *The Education of Henry Adams* . . .

```
                    Works Cited
Adams, Henry. The Education of Henry Adams:
      An Autobiography. Boston: Houghton, 1918.
      The American Studies Group at UVA
      Hypertext. Web. 6 Mar. 1998.
```

41. WWW—Online Scholarly Journal—MLA

Note: In "Tenure and Technology," Katz, Walker, and Cross argue . . .

Works Cited

Katz, Seth, Janice Walker, and Janet Cross.
    "Tenure and Technology: New Values,
    New Guidelines." *Kairos* 2.1 (1997): n.p.
    Web. 20 July 1997.

42. WWW—Online Popular Magazine—MLA

Note: Shafer claims in "The New Walter
Cronkite" that . . .

Works Cited

Shafer, Jack. "The New Walter Cronkite."
    Slate. Washington Post.Newsweek
    Interactive, 18 Oct. 1996. Web.
    12 July 1997.

43. WWW—Online Newspaper or Editorial—MLA

Note: Sue Ann Pressley suggests that the
movement to teach manners in school
is . . .

Works Cited

Pressley, Sue Ann. "Louisiana's Courtesy
    Call." *The Washington Post Online*.
    Washington Post, 5 Mar. 2000. Web. 6
    Mar. 2000.

Here's how to cite an online editorial. In this case, the date of
the editorial and the date of access to it are the same.

Note: In an editorial on 13 July 1997, the *New
York Times* . . .

Works Cited

"The Proved and the Unproved." Editorial.
    New York Times on the Web. New York
    Times, 13 July 1997. Web. 13 July
    1997.

44. **WWW—Personal Home Page—MLA**   Include the URL if it will help your readers locate the source.

Note: For an example of a digitally enhanced photograph, see the home page of Brett R. Elliott.

Works Cited

Elliott, Brett R. Home page. 4 Nov. 2004.
     Web. 5 Mar. 2005. <http://
     www.cwrl.utexas.edu/wcb/students/
     belliot5/belliot5.html>.

45. **Listserv/Newsgroup/Usenet Newsgroup—MLA**   Identify the author of the document or posting; put the subject line of the posting between quotation marks, followed by the words *Online posting*, the name of the listserv, the date the item was posted, the medium of publication (*Web*), and the date of access.

Note: Christy Heady recommends . . .

Works Cited

Heady, Christy. "Buy or Lease? Depends on How
     Long You'll Keep the Car." Online posting.
     ClariNet, 7 July 1997. Web. 14 July 1997.

Sometimes the name on a listserv may be incomplete or unconventional, but reproduce it just as it appears.

46. **Synchronous Communication (MOOs, MUDs)—MLA** Provide the speaker and/or site, the title of the session or event, the date of the session, the forum for the communication (if specified), the date of access, and the electronic address.

Note: In LinguaMOO, Inept_Guest observes . . .

Works Cited

Inept_Guest. Discussion of disciplinary
     politics in rhet/comp. *LinguaMOO*.
     Lingua, 12 Mar. 1998. Web. 12 Mar.
     1998.

47. Email—MLA

Note: Stratton makes the case that school vouchers would . . .

Works Cited

Stratton, Brad. "Re: the governor's school voucher plan." Message to the author. 1 Feb. 2005. E-mail.

48. CD-ROM/Diskette Database or Publication—MLA

To cite a CD-ROM or similar electronic database, provide basic information about the source itself—author, title, and publication information. Identify the name of the vendor if available (the vendor is the company publishing or distributing the database) and the date of electronic publication.

Note: (Bevington 98)

Works Cited

Bevington, David. "Castles in the Air: The Morality Plays." *The Theater of Medieval Europe: New Research in Early Drama*. Ed. Simon Eckchard. Cambridge: Cambridge UP, 1993. *MLA Bibliography*. CD-ROM. SilverPlatter. Feb. 1995.

For a CD-ROM database that is often updated (*ProQuest*, for example), you must provide publication dates for the item you are examining and for the data disk itself.

Note: (Alva 407–10)

Works Cited

Alva, Sylvia Alatore. "Differential Patterns of Achievement Among Asian-American Adolescents." *Journal of Youth and Adolescence* 22 (1993): 407–23. *Proquest General Periodicals*. CD-ROM. UMI-Proquest. June 1994.

Cite a book, encyclopedia, play, or other item published on CD-ROM or diskette just as if it were a printed source, adding the medium of publication (*Diskette* or *CD-ROM*, for example). When page numbers aren't available, use the author's name in the text of the paper to avoid parenthetical citation.

Note: `Bolter argues . . .`

Works Cited

`Bolter, Jay David.` *`Writing Space:`*
    `A Hypertext.` `Diskette. Hillsdale:`
    `Erlbaum, 1990.`

49. **Full-text Database Article—MLA** When you cite a source from an online database, follow the guidelines for citing works in print periodicals, but drop the original medium of publication (*Print*) and add the title of the database (italicized), the medium of publication (*Web*), and the date of access.

`Hart, Francis R. "The Spaces of Privacy:`
    `Jane Austen."` *`Nineteenth-Century`*
    `Fiction.` `30.3 (1975): 305-33.` *`JSTOR.`*
    `Web. 5 Feb. 2003.`

50. **Microfilm or Microfiche—MLA**

Note: `("How Long?" 434)`

Works Cited

`"How Long Will the Chemise Last?"`
    `Consumer Reports,` `Aug. 1958: 434-37.`
    `Microfilm.`

51. **Biblical Citation—MLA** Titles of sacred works, including all versions of the Bible, are not underlined.

Note: `(John 18:37-38)`

Works Cited

`The Jerusalem Bible. Ed. Alexander Jones.`
    `Garden City: Doubleday, 1966. Print.`

52. **Videotape/DVD—MLA**   Cite a video entry by title in most cases. You may include information about the producer, designer, performers, and so on. Identify the distributor, and provide a date.

Note: `Tae-Bo Workout` offers . . .

Works Cited

`Tae-Bo Workout: Instructional and Basic.`
        `Perf. Billy Blanks. Ventura, 1998.`
        `Videocassettes.`

Note: `The Matrix` DVD includes production notes that . . .

Works Cited

`The Matrix (Widescreen edition). Perf. Keanu`
        `Reeves and Laurence Fishburne. Warner,`
        `1999. DVD.`

53. **Movie—MLA**   In most cases, list a movie by its title. Provide information about actors, producers, and so on, to suit your readers. Identify the distributor, and give a date of production.

Note: In Lucas's film `American Graffiti` . . .

Works Cited

`American Graffiti. Dir. George Lucas. Perf.`
        `Richard Dreyfuss and Ron Howard.`
        `Universal, 1973. Film.`

54. **Television Program—MLA**

Note: In the episode "No Surrender, No Retreat" . . .

Works Cited

`"No Surrender, No Retreat." Dir. Mike Vejar.`
        `Writ. Michael Straczynski. Perf. Bruce`
        `Boxleitner, Claudia Christian, and Mira`
        `Furlan. Babylon 5. KEYE-42, Austin. 28`
        `July 1997. Television.`

55. Radio Program—MLA

Note: Early episodes of *Death Valley Days* . . .

Works Cited

Death Valley Days. Created by Ruth Cornwall
    Woodman. NBC Radio. WNBC, New York. 30
    Sept. 1930. Radio.

56. Personal Interview—MLA

Note: In an interview, Rev. Peter Gomes explains . . .

Works Cited

Gomes, Rev. Peter. Personal interview.
    23 Apr. 2004.

57. Musical Composition—MLA   List the work on the Works Cited page by the name of the composer. If you have sheet music or a score, give complete publication information. If you don't have a score or sheet music, provide a simpler entry.

Note: Scott Joplin published "The Strenuous
Life" at a time . . .

Works Cited

Joplin, Scott. "The Strenuous Life: A Ragtime
    Two Step." St. Louis: Stark, 1902.
    Print.

Note: Another Cole Porter song, "Too Darn
Hot" . . .

Works Cited

Porter, Cole. "Too Darn Hot." 1949.

58. Recording/Audio Clip—MLA

Note: An album such as *One Endless Night*
by Jimmie Dale Gilmore is a good example
of . . .

Works Cited

Gilmore, Jimmie Dale. *One Endless Night.*
        Windchanger/Rounder, 2000. CD.

Here is how to cite an audio clip from a Web site.

Note: The theme for NPR's *Car Talk*, "Dawgy
Mountain Breakdown" by David Grisman,
is . . .

Works Cited

Grisman, David. "Dawgy Mountain Breakdown."
        CarTalk at Cars.com. Natl. Public
        Radio. 1990. Web. 28 Feb. 2000.

59. **Speech—MLA**   If you have no printed text of the speech,
give the location and date of the address.

Note: Reagan explained his position in an address to . . .

Works Cited

Reagan, Ronald. "The Geneva Summit Meeting:
        A Measure of Progress." U.S. Congress,
        Washington, D.C. 21 Nov. 1985.
        Address.

With a printed text, give complete publication information.

Note: (O'Rourke 20)

Works Cited

O'Rourke, P. J. "Brickbats and Broomsticks."
        Capital Hilton, Washington, D.C. 2 Dec.
        1992. Rpt. *American Spectator* Feb. 1993:
        20-21. Print.

60. **Lecture—MLA**

Note: Addressing a conference of educators in
Cincinnati, William W. Cook . . .

Works Cited

Cook, William W. "Writing in the Spaces
        Left." Chair's Address. Conf. on Coll.
        Composition and Communication.
        Cincinnati. 19 Mar. 1992. Lecture.

61. Advertisement—MLA

Note: An advertisement for the Subaru Outback
sedan includes . . .

Works Cited

Subaru Outback. Advertisement. *Brill's
        Content* Feb. 2000: 37. Print.

List an online advertisement similarly. Provide an electronic
address and date of access.

Note: An Ameritrade Anniversary Offer
displays . . .

Works Cited

Ameritrade Anniversary Offer. Advertisement.
        Ameritrade.com. Ameritrade, 15 Mar.
        2000. Web. 15 Mar. 2000.

62. Letter—Published—MLA

Note: (Eliot 427)

Works Cited

Eliot, George. "To Thomas Clifford Allbutt."
        1 Nov. 1873. *Selections from George
        Eliot's Letters*. Ed. Gordon S. Haight.
        New Haven: Yale UP, 1985. 427. Print.

63. Letter—Unpublished—MLA

Note: In a letter to Agnes Weinstein dated 23
May 1917, Albert Newton complains . . .

Works Cited

Newton, Albert. Letter to Agnes Weinstein.
        23 May 1917. MS. Albert Newton Papers.
        Woodhill Lib., Cleveland.

64. **Artwork/Photograph—MLA**

> **Note:** The work resembles both the painting
> *Ariel* by Fuseli at the Folger and . . .

> Works Cited
>
> Fuseli, Henry. *Ariel*. Ca. 1800-1810. Oil on
>   canvas. Folger Shakespeare Lib.,
>   Washington, D.C.

65. **Drama or Play—MLA**   For printed texts, provide the usual Works Cited information. In parenthetical notes, give the act, scene, and line numbers when the work is so divided; give page numbers if it is not.

> **Note:** (*Ham.* 5.2.219-24)

> Works Cited
>
> Shakespeare, William. *The Tragedy of Hamlet,*
>   *Prince of Denmark*. Ed. Frank Kermode.
>   *The Riverside Shakespeare*. 2nd ed.
>   Ed. G. Blakemore Evans and J. J. M.
>   Tobin. Boston: Houghton, 1997.
>   1183-1245. Print.

> **Note:** (Stoppard 11-15)

> Works Cited
>
> Stoppard, Tom. *Rosencrantz and Guildenstern*
>   *Are Dead*. New York: Grove, 1967.

For performances of plays, give the title, the author, and then any specific information that seems relevant—director, performers, producers, set designer, theater company, and so on. Conclude the entry with a theater, location, and date.

> **Note:** In a rare and memorable performance of
> Shakespeare's *Timon of Athens* . . .

> Works Cited
>
> *Timon of Athens*. By William Shakespeare. Dir.
>   Michael Benthall. Perf. Ralph Richardson,
>   Paul Curran, and Margaret Whiting. Old
>   Vic, London. 5 Sept. 1956. Performance.

d Sample MLA Paper

MLA does not require a separate cover sheet or title page. If your instructor expects one, center the title of your paper and your name in the upper third of the sheet. Center the course title, your instructor's name, and the date of submission in the lower third of the sheet, double-spacing between the elements.

The first page of a paper without a separate title page will look like the sample on page 99. Check the following items when preparing your project.

- Number each page in the upper right-hand corner, one-half inch from the top, one inch from the right margin. Precede the page number with your last name.
- On the first page, place your name, your instructor's name, the course title, and the date in the upper left-hand corner, beginning one inch from the top of the page. Double-space these items.
- Center the title a double space under the date. Capitalize the first and last word of the title. Capitalize all other words *except* articles (*a, an, the*), prepositions, the *to* in infinitives, and coordinating conjunctions—unless they are the first or last words.
- Do not underline or boldface the title. Do not use all caps, place the title between quotation marks, or end it with a period. Titles may, however, end with question marks or include words or phrases that are italicized, underlined, or between quotation marks.

RIGHT   Violence in Shakespeare's *Macbeth*

RIGHT   Dylan's "Like a Rolling Stone" Revisited

- Begin the body of the essay a double space below the title. Double-space the entire paper, including quotations.
- Use one-inch margins at the sides and bottom of each page.

General formatting guidelines for MLA in-text citations are given on page 73 and for the Works Cited list on page 74.

Ben H. Brenneman

Professor Ruszkiewicz

Rhetoric 306

2 March 2004

Can Quality Survive the Standardized Test?

¶1 In *Seeking Diversity*, a book on teaching middle school language arts, author and teacher Linda Rief says, "I expect good reading and writing, in which process and product are woven tightly into literate tapestries of wonder and awe" (10). Rief thus describes the Holy Grail of writing instruction: a classroom in which students learn to write because they care about the final product and want to do excellent work. Such an environment would teach students the ability to write by turning them into writers. Unfortunately, the American education system today is failing to teach many students even the basic skills they will need to survive. Statements by teachers that "the greater number of the young people we teach . . . do not know how to read, spell, write, use correct grammar, do simple math, remember, use logic" are supported by statistics showing that "only 55% of the nation's 17-year-olds and 49% of out-of-school adults are able to write an acceptable letter ordering a product by mail" (Neill 18). Yet the dominant response to this problem--competency testing in our public schools--may be destroying any regard students may have for language by turning writing into a formulaic exercise.

¶2 Many states, in fact, have already responded to problems in their educational

Brenneman 2

systems by passing laws mandating the skills that students must learn by a specified grade. The students' ability to reach the objectives and the faculty's ability to teach this "standards-based curriculum" are then measured by statewide standardized tests. Students and schools that fall short of the mark can then be identified for improvement. As Neill explains, "the strongest argument in support of competency requirements is the potential for motivating students, schools, and districts" (8). The results of testing are carefully monitored and publicized to show continuing improvement in the performance of public schools (see Table 1).

Table 1

Percentage of Students Passing All Texas Assessment of Academic Skills Exams (TAAS)

	1994	1995	1996	1997	1998	1999	2000
Grade 3	58	66	70	74	76	78	76
Grade 4	54	64	67	72	78	78	80
Grade 5	58	66	73	79	83	82	85
Grade 6	56	60	69	77	79	79	81
Grade 7	55	58	67	75	78	77	79
Grade 8	49	50	59	67	72	76	77
Grade 10	52	54	60	68	72	75	80

Source: Texas Business and Education Coalition.
    School Improvement Since TBEC Began. 2000.
    Web. 24 Sept. 2004.

¶3   In many states this progress has been motivated by attaching increasingly serious consequences to the results of these tests.

Students who fail the state aptitude test may be held back a grade, or they may even be denied a high school diploma. Teachers are also under increasing pressure to get test scores up. Jack Kaufhold, a professor of educational psychology, notes that principals have been warned, "If your test scores don't go up, you may lose your job." He adds, "Teachers also know that if their students' achievement test scores fluctuate too much from year to year, they too could be demoted or dismissed" (14).

¶4   State officials justify these types of high-stakes assessment on the grounds that the skills the tests focus on are those students will need to function in society. They argue, moreover, that students who receive a quality education should have little trouble fulfilling the minimum requirements. For instance, the standards for writing set in Texas, called the "Texas Essential Knowledge and Skills" or TEKS, state that students who graduate high school must "write in a variety of forms using effective word choice, structure, and sentences with an emphasis on organizing logical arguments . . . ; write in a voice and style appropriate to audience and purpose; and organize in writing to ensure coherence" ("Chapters"). In other words, everyone who receives a high school diploma should be able to communicate effectively in writing. Students demonstrate their skill during the Texas Assessment of Academic Skills (TAAS), by composing an essay. As Mary argues, on a WWW forum sponsored by *Teachers.Net*, "The TEKS

based TAAS are a reflection of the specific
standards the children of our state should
meet. That's precisely what we should be
teaching." Many teachers, however, find that
their curriculums are already adequate. Their
response to these requirements is like teacher
M. E. Castillo's: "If I'm teaching them well,
my students tend to do fine on the tests
without much special preparation." Rief, for
example, gives her students "a two-day crash
course . . . just before they take the
state-mandated achievement tests. . . . Two
days is all I allow" (180).

¶5   Unfortunately some schools fall short
of the mark. The administrators in these
institutions are then forced to make changes
to the curriculum in order to raise scores
quickly. In Maryland teachers responded to a
writing test that they felt was too difficult
by creating writing labs, increasing the
amount of writing done in regular English, and
cooperating between departments to focus on
writing in all disciplines (Corbett and
Wilson). This is the type of reform the tests
were intended to produce. The instructors at
this school improved their curriculum by finding
innovative ways to teach their students how
to write. Anne Shaughnessy, when preparing her
students for the Florida assessment, had them
discuss their responses to a sample prompt. She
showed them that the qualities they felt made
an essay successful were the same criteria that
would be used to score their tests. She then
had them use the actual rubric to score their
essays in class. In this way Shaughnessy gave

her students some insight into the logic behind
the test, making it more than simply an arbitrary
exercise. She writes, "Clearly I was teaching
to the test, but I was also introducing
activities that extended rather than displaced
the writing curriculum" (56).

¶6   These improvements are certainly
commendable. They occur when schools are blessed
with creative teachers who are willing to take
risks. However, many educators, when faced with
the possibility of unemployment, turn to the
tried-and-true method the army uses to train new
recruits: drill, drill, drill. In the Maryland
case, for example, Corbett and Wilson note that
"teachers would stop what they were doing with
students . . . and inject an intense period
of . . . 'drill and review' specifically related
to the test" (124). When preparing for a writing
exam, students spend this period responding to
practice prompts, often from previous tests that
have been released by the state. A teacher in
Texas reported that she "had to give a writing
test AND a reading test every six weeks"
(Melissa). In teaching circles this strategy is
known as the "drill-and-kill" approach. In other
words, students are drilled until all genuine
interest in the subject is killed by weeks of
prompt writing.

¶7   Teachers are alarmed by the drill-and-kill
approach to test preparation. They fear that
the focus of their instruction has shifted from
producing excellent writing for a general
audience to producing adequate writing in order
to avoid the wrath of the state. This attitude
is communicated to the students simply by the

time spent in practice. As one Texas teacher laments, "from mid-January through April we are not teachers, we are masters of how to take a test" (Linda/tx). In this environment students begin to believe that mastery of the test is the goal of their education. They often create, or are even taught, ways to improve their scores by manipulating the test. According to Donna Garner, any student who got a high score on the essay portion of the TAAS could miss most of the questions on the grammar-oriented part of the test and still pass. She says that, unfortunately "Once the students learn to 'play the TAAS game' by scripting their essays to a set pattern, the accuracy of the content is of little importance to them." These students see writing as a task they will have to perform once in order to graduate, not as a skill they will need to communicate effectively in the real world.

¶8   Kaufhold descries this mindset as "convergent thinking." He says that these types of tests emphasize "the need to search for *one right answer*. Creative ideas or divergent thinking is discouraged as students narrow the scope of their thinking toward what will be on the test" (14). Ironically, such narrowing is actually endorsed by A. D. Rison in his 1990 book designed to help students pass the language arts portion of the TAAS. He supports the use of a "Rison Design," basically the typical hourglass shape long used to teach the five-paragraph theme. He believes that students should use this design so that "many competing functions, thinking, writing, vision, and other

Brenneman 7

unnecessary movements are lessened" (136). And yet for years, many teachers of composition have complained that such a standard form "almost inevitably encourages dull, formulaic writing" (Irmscher 97) and that, when these forms are taught, "all of the students seemed to write exactly alike" (104). By focusing on formulaic essays, teachers encourage convergent thinking by giving students the impression that there is only one correct way to write. In a 1990 article printed by the *English Journal*, John Dinan says that students "believe that barren, formulaic writing is what we want from them. Standardized tests of English cultivate this belief . . . because they implicitly define the writing process as mechanistic and impersonal" (54). The concept of writing as a mechanical process is very different from that advocated in Rief's ideal classroom.

¶9   As dull as these exercises are for teachers to grade, they are even duller for students to write. Rief makes the comment, "I cannot immerse my students in literature I don't like, any more than any of us can write effectively on topics in which we have little interest" (19). One of the sample prompts Rison gives for fourth graders consists of a picture of a man sitting in a hole eating a sandwich. Beside him lie a pick and a lunchbox. The caption says, "This is a picture of a construction worker. Look at this picture and describe what you see on two sheets" (143). Is this topic supposed to produce a student's best writing? Are there aspects of a construction worker's life to which fourth graders can relate their own

experiences? Why should they care about the
construction worker at all? Nothing in this
exercise has any application beyond preparation
for answering similarly bland test prompts in
the future. When confronted with one such
prompt, Rief cut it out of the test books for
her class and replaced it with "Write about
anything you care deeply about. Try to convince
the reader how much you care" (121).

¶10   The prompts Rison gives for tenth graders
are not much better: "Your school wants to add
a new course. Your principal has asked for
suggestions. Write a letter to your principal
telling what courses you would add and give
convincing reasons for your choice" (180). The
work can seem mindless. Students in Maryland
were forced to sit through drill sessions even
after they had passed the state-mandated tests
for graduation (Corbett). Imagine, day after
day of tedious prompt writing for no purpose
whatsoever. No wonder Dinan complains,

> [m]ost students simply don't *like*
> writing very much, they are apprehensive
> about it, beleaguered by it, inclined to
> do it only on demand. (55)

Drilling students for these tests undermines
the writing teacher's attempts to create an
environment in which students are interested in
and feel comfortable with their writing.

¶11   Under these conditions students learn to
hate writing. They see it as a boring chore, a
task they must complete in order to please a
higher authority rather than a process intended
to produce something they themselves can take

pride in. As soon as they learn to write the type of dry, five-paragraph essay that puts professors to sleep, their growth as writers ends. The type of idyllic writing classroom Rief describes is still possible under the pressure of a high-stakes test, but it requires creative faculty willing to bet their jobs that students can pass these tests without drills. Unfortunately, when superintendents are receiving calls from angry parents whose children aren't going to graduate, what is good can take a back seat to what is expedient. In the rush to raise the scores of those who can't meet the state objectives, creativity is crushed in those who can.

Works Cited

Castillo, M.E. Personal Interview 13 Jul. 2004.

"Chapters 110 and 128, Subchapter C." *Texas
      Education Agency Administrative Rules*.
      Texas Education Agency. 1 Sept. 1998. Web.
      6 March 2000.

Corbett, H. Dickson, and Bruce L. Wilson.
      Testing, Reform, and Rebellion. Norwood:
      Ablex, 1991. Print.

Dinan, John. "Standardized Tests: Multiple
      Choices of the Wrong Kind." *English Journal*
      79.3 (Oct. 1990): 54-56. Print.

Garner, Donna. "RE: A Special Note on the TAAS
      Series." Online posting. 29 Jan. 2000.
      EducationNews.org Bulletin Board. Education
      News. Web. 13 Feb. 2000.

Irmscher, William F. *Teaching Expository Writing*.
      New York: Holt, 1979. Print.

Kaufhold, Jack. "What's Wrong with Teaching
      for the Test?" *The School Administrator* 55.4
      (Dec. 1998): 14-16. Print.

Linda/tx. "RE: Teaching to the TAAS Criticism
      Getting to Me." Online posting. 4 Feb. 2000.
      Texas Teachers Chatboard.
      Texas.Teachers.Net. Web. 13 Feb. 2000.

Mary. "RE: Teaching to the TAAS Criticism
      Getting to Me." Online posting. 4 Feb.
      2000. *Texas Teachers Chatboard*.
      Texas.Teachers.Net. Web. 13 Feb. 2000.

Melissa. "RE: Does Your School Give a Released
      TAAS Test?" Online posting. 14 Jan.
      2000. *Texas Teachers Chatboard*.
      Texas.Teachers.Net. Web. 13 Feb. 2000.

Brenneman 11

Neill, Shirley Boes. *The Competency Movement:
    Problems and Solutions*. Sacramento, CA:
    Educational News Service, 1978. Print.

Rief, Linda. *Seeking Diversity*. Portsmouth:
    Heinemann, 1992. Print.

Rison, A. D. *A. D. Rison's Teachers' and Parents'
    Guide to Pass the TAAS Test: Language Arts,
    Reading and Writing*. Austin: Sunbelt, 1990.
    Print.

Shaughnessy, Anne. "Teaching to the Test:
    Sometimes a Good Practice." *English Journal*
    83.2 (Apr. 1994): 54–56. Print.

12 APA Style

"The imagination imitates. It is the critical spirit that creates."

—OSCAR WILDE, playwright, poet, novelist

The American Psychological Association (APA) style of documentation is used in many social sciences and related courses. The basic procedures for using APA style are spelled out in this chapter. A full explanation of APA procedures is provided by the *Publication Manual of the American Psychological Association,* 6th edition (2010), and in the *APA Style Guide to Electronic References* (2007). The APA Web site at <http://www.apa.org/> offers students software to assist in creating APA style papers.

EXPRESS!

You need to take only two steps to use APA style properly.

1. Insert an in-text note for each source you use in your project.
2. Record all sources used in these notes in a References page.

Notice in the following example how the in-text note tells readers to look for a work by Tebeaux published in 1991 on the References page.

```
Tebeaux (1991) argues that technical writing
developed in important ways during the
English Renaissance.
```

Your readers can then turn to the References page for complete publication information about the source.

```
                    References
Tebeaux, E. (1991). Ramus, visual rhetoric,
        and the emergence of page design in
        medical writing of the English
        Renaissance. Written Communication,
        8, 411-445.
```

In-Text Citations

The main purpose of the in-text citation is to direct your reader to the original source of the information you are citing. See 11c, APA Models, for numerous examples of in-text notes and their corresponding References entries. For formatting of in-text notes, see "In-Text Citations: APA Style," page 113.

1. **A work that includes an author and page number**

   Most commonly, the APA note consists of the last name of the source's author, followed immediately by the year the material was published, in parentheses. Alternately, you can place both the author's last name and the date within the parentheses.

   ```
   Tebeaux (1991) argues that technical writing
   developed in important ways during the
   English Renaissance.
   ```

   ```
   Technical writing developed in important
   ways during the English Renaissance (Tebeaux,
   1991).
   ```

   You must include a page number for direct quotations, and you may choose to do so for indirect citations as well.

   ```
   During the English Renaissance, writers began
   to employ "various page design strategies
   to enhance visual access" (Tebeaux, 1991,
   p. 413).
   ```

   You may also distribute the citation information throughout.

   ```
   Tebeaux (1991) observes that for writers in
   the late sixteenth century, the philosophical
   ideas of Peter Ramus "provided a significant
   impetus to major changes in page design"
   (p. 413).
   ```

2. **More than one work written by an author in a single year**

   Assign a lowercase letter after the date to distinguish between the two works.

   ```
   (Rosner, 2003a)
   ```

   ```
   (Rosner, 2003b)
   ```

The charge is raised by Rosner (2003a),
quickly answered by Anderson (2003), and then
raised again by Rosner (2003b).

3. **More than one work in a single note**

   Separate the citations with a semicolon and list them in alphabetical order.

   (Searle, 1993; Yamibe, 2004)

4. **A whole Web site**

   When referring to an entire Web site or home page (rather than an individual posting, internal page, or section), give the name of the site in your signal phrase followed by its Internet addess in parentheses (for the first reference only).

   The U.S. Census Bureau regularly publishes statistics on home purchases (http://www.census
   .gov), along with other demographic data.

5. **Two or more sources in a single sentence**

   Insert the notes directly after the statements they support.

   While Porter (1981) suggests that the ecology
   of the aquifer might be hardier than
   suspected, "given the size of the drainage
   area and the nature of the subsurface rock"
   (p. 62), there is no reason to believe that
   the county needs another shopping mall in an
   area described as "one of the last outposts
   of undisturbed nature in the state"
   (Martinez, 1982, p. 28).

6. **A single source provides a series of references**

   There is no need to repeat the name of the author until other sources interrupt the series. After the first reference, use only page numbers until another citation intervenes. Even then, if the references all occur in a single paragraph, repeat only the author's last name (without the date).

   The council vetoed zoning approval for a mall
   in an area described by Martinez (1982) as
   the last outpost of undisturbed nature in the
   state. The area provides a "unique
   environment for several endangered species

of birds and plant life" (p. 31). The birds, especially the endangered vireo, require breeding spaces free from encroaching development (Harrison & Cafiero, 1979). Rare plant life is similarly endangered (Martinez).

7. **Quotations of forty words or more**

Indent a long quotation five spaces from the left margin, omit quotation marks, and place the parenthetical note outside the final punctuation mark.

Mansfield (1998) explains this effect of trauma on cognition:

> During normal experience, literal images are evaluated for meaning, placed in a narrative, and stripped of extraneous information. The symbolic image that results contains only the details that are essential for the memory to make sense. During a traumatic experience this processing is impaired. (p. 4)

In-Text Citations: APA Style

- A comma and a space separate the author's last name and the date of publication: (Martinez, 1982)
- The abbreviation *p.* or *pp.* and a space precede a page number or numbers: (Martinez, 1982, p. 31)
- If the source has two authors, their last names are joined by an ampersand: (Harrison & Cafiero, 2004)
- If you need to cite more than one work written by an author in a single year, assign a lowercase letter after the date to distinguish between the author's two works: (Rosner, 2003a), (Rosner, 2003b)
- The note itself falls *outside* the quotation marks: " . . . " (Rosner, 2003a)
- The final punctuation for the sentence comes *after* the note: (Rosner, 2003b).*

*Exception: If a quotation is forty words or longer, see #7, above.

b The References Page

On a separate page at the end of your project, list alphabetically every source you used directly, except for personal communications. Title the list "References."

References Page: APA Style

- Center the title "References" at the top of the page, with no quotation marks.
- Arrange the items alphabetically by the last name of the author. Give initials only for first names. If no author is given, list the work according to the first word in the title (excluding *The, A,* and *An*).
- List two or more entries by the same author by year of publication, from earliest to latest. If one author publishes two works in the same year, list them alphabetically by title.
- Make first line of each entry flush with the left-hand margin. Subsequent lines in an entry are indented five spaces.
- Double-space the list. Students are permitted to single-space individual entries, but the double space is preserved between entries.
- Punctuate items carefully. Remember that a period ends each entry—except those that terminate with an electronic address.
- Capitalize only the first word and any proper names in the title of a book or article. Within a title, capitalize the first word after a colon.
- When an electronic source includes a DOI (Digital Object Identifier), use the DOI in place of a URL.

```
                          Genome Project    10
                    References
Cohen, J. Venter's Genome Sheds New Light
     on Human Variation. (2007). Science,
     317, 1311.
Pennisi, E. Working the (Gene Count)
     Numbers: Finally, a Firm Answer?
     (2007) Science, 316, 1113.
     http://www.sciencemag.org/cgi
     /content/summary/316/5828/1113a
Yesley, M. S. What's ELSI got to do with
     it? Bioethics and the Human Genome
```

Project. (2008). *New Genetics & Society*, 27, 1-6. doi: 10.1080/14636770701843527.

Zwart, Ni. H. Genomics and self-knowledge: implications for societal research and debate. (2007). *New Genetics & Society*, 26(2), 181-202. doi: 10.1080/14636770701466881.

c APA Models

Following you will find APA models for creating in-text notes and the corresponding References entries for numerous kinds of sources. Simply locate the type of source you need to cite in the APA Models Index and then locate that item by number in the list that follows.

APA Models Index

66. Book, One Author—APA

Notes:

Kauffman (2004) found . . .

(Kauffman, 2004)

(Kauffman, 2004, p. 62)

References

Kauffman, J. (2004). *Cases in emotional and behavioral disorders of children and youth.* Upper Saddle River, NJ: Prentice Hall.

67. Book, Two Authors—APA

Notes:

Lasswell and Kaplan (1950) found . . .

(Lasswell & Kaplan, 1950)

(Lasswell & Kaplan, 1950, pp. 210-213)

References

Lasswell, H. D., & Kaplan, A. (1950). *Power and society: A framework for political inquiry.* New York, NY: Yale University Press.

68. Book, Three or More Authors—APA

First note: Rosenberg, Gerver, & Howton (1971) found . . .

Subsequent notes: Rosenberg et al. (1971) found . . .

First note: (Rosenberg, Gerver, & Howton, 1971)

Subsequent notes: (Rosenberg et al., 1971)

References

Rosenberg, B., Gerver, I., & Howton, F. W. (1971). *Mass society in crisis: Social problems and social pathology* (2nd ed.). New York, NY: Macmillan.

Provide surnames and initials for up to seven authors, with an ampersand between the last two names; for works with eight or more authors, list the first six authors' names, then insert three ellipses, then add the *last* author's name.

69. Book, Revised—APA

Notes:

```
Edelmann (1969) found . . .
(Edelmann, 1969)
(Edelmann, 1969, p. 62)
```

```
                References
Edelmann, A. T. (1969). Latin American
        government and politics (Rev. ed.).
        Homewood, IL: Dorsey.
```

70. Book, Edited—APA

Notes:

```
Journet and Kling (1984) observe . . .
(Journet & Kling, 1984)
```

```
                References
Journet, D., & Kling, J. (Eds.). (1984).
        Readings for technical writers.
        Glenview, IL: Scott, Foresman.
```

71. Book, No Author—APA

Notes:

```
In Illustrated Atlas (1985) . . .
(Illustrated Atlas, 1985, pp. 88-89)
```

```
                References
Illustrated atlas of the world. (1985).
        Chicago, IL: Rand McNally.
```

When the author of a work is actually listed as "Anonymous," cite the work that way in the References list and parenthetical note.

```
(Anonymous, 1995)
```

72. Book, a Collection or Anthology—APA

Notes:

Feinstein (1967) found . . .

(Feinstein, 1967)

References

Feinstein, C. H. (Ed.). (1967). *Socialism, capitalism, and economic growth.* Cambridge, England: Cambridge University Press.

73. Work Within a Collection, Anthology, or Reader—APA
List the item on the References page by the author of the piece you are actually citing, not the editor(s) of the collection.

Notes:

Patel (1967) found . . .

(Patel, 1967)

References

Patel, S. (1967). World economy in transition (1850-2060). In C. H. Feinstein (Ed.), *Socialism, capitalism, and economic growth* (pp. 255-270). Cambridge, England: Cambridge University Press.

74. Chapter in a Book—APA

Notes:

Clark (1969) observes . . .

(Clark, 1969)

References

Clark, K. (1969). Heroic materialism. In *Civilisation* (pp. 321-347). New York, NY: HarperCollins.

75. Book Review—APA

Notes:

Max (1999) claims . . .

(Max, 1999)

References

Max, D. T. (1999, December 27). All the
      world's an I.P.O.: Shakespeare the
      profiteer [Review of the book
      Shakespeare's 21st-century economics:
      The morality of love and money]. *The New*
      York Observer, p. 35.

If a review is untitled, identify the author and date and
describe the item in brackets.

Notes:

Farquhar (1987) observes . . .

(Farquhar, 1987)

References

Farquhar, J. (1987). [Review of the book
      Medical power and social knowledge].
      American Journal of Psychology, 94, 256.

76. **Article in a Scholarly Journal—APA**   Scholarly journals are
    usually identified by volume number or season (rather than day,
    week, or month of publication) and are paginated year by year,
    with a full year's work gathered and treated as a volume. Include
    BOTH volume and issue number ONLY if the journal is
    paginated by issue. Cite articles from such scholarly journals
    by providing author, date, title of article, journal, volume, and
    page numbers.

Notes:

Tebeaux (1991) observes . . .

(Tebeaux, 1991, p. 411)

References

Tebeaux, E. (1991). Ramus, visual rhetoric, and
      the emergence of page design in medical
      writing of the English Renaissance.
      Written Communication, 8, 411-445.

77. **Article in a Monthly Periodical—APA**

Notes:

Greenstein (2000) notes . . .

(Greenstein, 2000)

References

Greenstein, J. (2000, February). Snow job.
    Brill's Content, 3, 70-77.

78. **Article in a Weekly or Biweekly Periodical—APA**

    Notes:

    Lasch-Quinn (2000) observes . . .

    (Lasch-Quinn, 2000)

    (Lasch-Quinn, 2000, p. 37)

References

Lasch-Quinn, E. (2000, March 6). Mothers
    and markets. *The New Republic, 222*,
    37-44.

79. **Article in a Newsletter—APA**

    Notes:

    Piedmont-Marton (1997) argues . . .

    (Piedmont-Marton, 1997)

References

Piedmont-Marton, E. (1997, July 20).
    Schoolmarms or language paramedics? *The
    Writer's Block, 4*, 6.

80. **Article in a Periodical, Author Not Named—APA**

    Notes:

    In "Aladdin releases" (1993) . . .

    ("Aladdin releases," 1993)

References

Aladdin releases desktop tools. (1993,
    October). *Macworld, 10*, 35.

81. **Newspaper Article, Author Named—APA**   If the article
    does not appear on consecutive pages in the newspaper, give
    all the page numbers. Abbreviations for *page* (*p.*) and *pages*
    (*pp.*) are used with newspaper entries.

    Notes:

    Bragg (1994) reports . . .

    (Bragg, 1994, p. 7A)

References

Bragg, R. (1994, October 15). Weather gurus
going high-tech. *San Antonio Express-
News,* pp. 1A, 7A.

82. Newspaper Article, Author Not Named—APA

Notes:

In the article "Scientists find" (1994) . . .
("Scientists find," 1994)

References

Scientists find new dinosaur species in
Africa. (1994, October 14). *The Daily
Texan,* p. 3.

83. Computer Software—APA   List authors only when they
own the product.

Note:

In Adobe Pagemill (1995) . . .

References

Adobe Pagemill 1.0 [Computer software]. (1995).
Mountain View, CA: Adobe Systems.

**84. Online Source, Archived Listserv, or Usenet Newsgroup—
APA**   List the author(s), date of publication or posting (if
available), the title of the source (italicized, unless an article), and online retrieval information, including the Web
address (or URL) of the source. If the site housing the
source provides a DOI, list it instead of retrieval date and
URL or database. If the site lists no DOI, search for one at
<http://www.crossref.org/guestquery/>. When giving a DOI,
omit all other online retrieval information and preface the
DOI with doi:.

Notes:

Dubrowski (1994) reports . . .
(Dubrowski, 1994)

References

Dubrowski, J. (1994, October 18). Mixed
signals from Washington leave

```
automakers puzzled. Retrieved from
C-reuters@clarinet.com.
```

85. **WWW Page—Generic—APA**

Notice that in APA, angle brackets are not used to mark URLs

Notes:

```
Silver (2009) explains . . .
(Silver, 2009)
```

```
                    References
Silver, N. FiveThirtyEight: Politics Done
        Right. (2009) Retrieved from
        http://www.fivethirtyeight.com
```

86. **WWW Page—Online Scholarly Article—APA**

No bracketed explanation of the medium is necessary.

Notes:

```
Yelsey (2008) reports . . .
(Yelsey, 2008)
```

```
                    References
Yesley, M. S. What's ELSI got to do with it?
        Bioethics and the Human Genome Project.
        (2008). New Genetics & Society, 27, 1-6.
        doi: 10.1080/14636770701843527
```

87. **WWW Page—Online Newspaper Article—APA**

Notes:

```
Cohen (1997) asks . . .
(Cohen, 1997)
```

```
                    References
Cohen, E. (1997, January 17). Shrinks aplenty
        online but are they credible? The New
        York Times on the Web. Retrieved from
        http://search.nytimes.com/search
```

88. WWW Page—Online Abstract—APA

Notes:

Maddux and Galinsky (2009) report . . .

(Maddux and Galinsky, 2009)

References

Maddux, W. W. and A. D. Galinsky. Cultural
borders and mental barriers: the
relationship between living abroad
and creativity. *Journal of Personality
and Social Psychology*, 96, 1047-61.
doi: 10.1037/a0014861

89. Email—APA   Electronic communications not stored or archived have limited use for researchers. APA style treats such information (as well as email) like personal communication. Make no mention of these sources in the References list. However, acknowledge them in the body of the essay in parenthetical notes.

According to Rice (personal communication,
October 14, 2004) . . .

90. Movie/Videotape/DVD—APA   This is also the basic form for audiotapes, slides, charts, and other nonprint sources. The specific medium is described between brackets, as shown here for a film.

Notes:

McCanlies (1998) features . . .

(McCanlies, 1998)

References

McCanlies, T. (Screenwriter). (1998).
Dancer, Texas [Film]. Culver City, CA:
TriStar.

91. Musical Recording—APA

Note:

```
In the song "What Was It You Wanted?" (Dylan,
1989, track 10) . . .
```

```
                    References
Dylan, B. (1989). What was it you wanted?
      [Recorded by Willie Nelson]. On Across the
      borderline [CD]. New York, NY: Columbia.
```

d Sample APA Pages

For a sample References list, see page 114. To view complete research papers in APA style, visit *The Undergraduate Journal of Psychology*, an online psychology journal for undergraduates, at <http:/www.psych.uncc.edu/Journal.htm>.

1. Title page

APA style requires a separate title page; use the model below and review the following checklist.

- Type your paper on white bond paper. Preferred typefaces (when you have a choice) include Times Roman, American Typewriter, and Courier.
- Number the title page and all subsequent pages in the upper right-hand corner. For an article that will be published, indicate at the top of the page what the running head for the essay should be in all caps, preceded by "Runing head:" (this label should only appear on the title page). Put the same running head in the upper margin of all subsequent pages.
- Center the title, your name (first name, middle initial, last name), and your school name as shown in the model.

```
Running head: TEST ANXIETY                        1


   The Relationship Between Test Anxiety, Sleep
  Habits, and Self-perceived Academic Competency
         Chad S. Briggs and Fred Ribich
              Wartburg College
```

- In the title, capitalize all important words and all words of four letters or more. Do not underline or boldface the title, and do not use all capitals.

2. **Abstract**

   An abstract is a concise summary of the paper. Abstracts are common in papers using APA style. When preparing an abstract, consult the following model and review the following checklist.

   - Place the abstract on a separate page, after the title page.
   - Center the word "Abstract" at the top of the page, without quotation marks.
   - Include the running head and put the page number (2) in the upper right-hand corner.
   - Double-space the abstract.
   - Do not indent the first line; type the abstract in block form.
   - Strict APA form limits abstracts to 960 characters or fewer (about 120 words).

TEST ANXIETY   2

                          Abstract

One hundred fifty-eight college students
completed questionnaires and tests that measure
test anxiety, sleep habits, and self-perceived
academic competency. It was hypothesized that
test anxiety and irregular sleep patterns will
lower college students' self-perceived academic
competency. The results showed that high test
anxiety and poor sleep habits negatively affected
students' self-perceived academic competency. It
was also found that high self-perceived academic
competency was positively correlated with GPA (a
measure of performance). This study shows the
need for further research that deals with the
relationship between self-perceived academic
competency and academic performance. This will
enable professionals to look at another variable
that affects academic performance in more detail.

13 Chicago Style

"To a historian, libraries are food, shelter, and even muse."

—BARBARA TUCHMAN, historian

Writers who prefer full footnotes or endnotes rather than in-text notes often use the "humanities style" of documentation recommended in *The Chicago Manual of Style* (15th ed., 2003). Basic procedures for this system are spelled out in this chapter. If you need further information or prefer the author-date style of Chicago documentation, consult the full manual or *A Manual for Writers of Term Papers, Theses, and Dissertations* (6th ed., 1996). For answers to general questions about editing, or Chicago style specifically, check out the FAQ supported by the manuscript editing department at the University of Chicago Press at <http://www.press.uchicago.edu/Misc/Chicago/cmosfaq/cmosfaq.html>.

EXPRESS!

You need to take only three basic steps to use Chicago style properly.

1. Place a raised number after any sentence or clause you need to document.
2. Link every note number to a note.
3. Record all sources in a bibliographic list. (This step is sometimes optional; consult your instructor.)

The raised (superscript number) after the quotation in the following example leads the reader to a corresponding note 1.

```
Athena gives Diomedes "courage and boldness,
to make him come to the front and cover
himself in glory."1
```

To find complete publication information, your readers can then turn to note 1.

```
1. Homer, The Iliad, trans. Robert Fitzgerald
(New York: Anchor Press, 1974), 58.
```

Chicago Style allows you to use either footnotes (at the bottom of the page) or endnotes (at the end of the paper), although you must be consistent throughout your paper; the two types of notes can't be mixed.

If a bibliographic list—Works Cited or Bibliography—is also required, your reader will find similar information in a slightly different format there.

```
Homer, The Iliad. Translated by Robert
     Fitzgerald. New York: Anchor Press,
     1974.
```

Chicago allows for two styles of bibliography pages: Works Cited or Bibliography. If you will list only the sources directly cited in your project, use the term "Works Cited" to head your references list. If you will list all the sources you consulted in your research, use the term "Bibliography."

a In-Text Citations and Notes

The purpose of the in-text citation is to direct your reader to the note, which includes the original source of the information you are citing. In the text, place a raised (superscript) number after the material you need to document. The numbers run consecutively throughout the paper. (To create such a raised number, select "superscript" from your word-processing font options.) See 13c, Chicago Models, for examples of notes. For formatting of in-text citations and notes, see "In-Text Citations and Notes: Chicago Style," pages 128–29.

1. **Two or more sources in a single sentence**

   The note numbers appear right after the statements they support.

```
While some in the humanities fear that
electronic technologies may make the "notion
of wisdom" obsolete,2 others suggest that
technology must be the subject of serious
study even in elementary and secondary
school.3
```

   The notes for this sentence would appear as follows.

```
     2. Sven Birkerts, The Gutenberg Elegies:
The Fate of Reading in an Electronic Age
(Boston: Faber and Faber, 1994), 139.
```

> 3. Neil Postman, "The Word Weavers/The World Makers," in *The End of Education: Redefining the Value of School* (New York: Alfred A. Knopf, 1995), 172-93.

Observe that note 2 documents a particular quotation, whereas note 3 refers to a full book chapter.

2. **One work several times in a project**

The first note gives full information about author(s), title, and publication.

> 1. Helen Wilkinson, "It's Just a Matter of Time," *Utne Reader* (May/June 1995): 66-67.

Then, in shorter papers, any subsequent citations require only the last name of the author(s) and page number(s).

> 3. Wilkinson, 66.

In longer papers, the entry may also include a shortened title to make references from page to page easier to follow.

> 3. Wilkinson, "Matter of Time," 66.

If you cite the same work again immediately after a full note, you may use the Latin abbreviation *Ibid.* (meaning "in the same place"), followed by the page number(s) of the citation.

> 1. James Morgan, "Blue Highways," in *The Distance to the Moon* (New York: Riverhead, 1999), 93.
>
> 2. Ibid., 89.

To avoid using *Ibid.* when documenting the same source in succession, simply use a page reference—for example, (89)—within the text itself. When successive citations are to exactly the same page, *Ibid.* alone can be used.

In-Text Citations and Notes: Chicago Style

- Raised numbers in the text follow any punctuation marks, except for dashes: ". . . with glory."[6]
- Place notes either at the bottom of each page (footnotes), or in a single list titled "Notes" at the end of your paper (endnotes).
- Single-space individual notes, and double-space between notes.
- Indent the first line of each note like a paragraph.

- Use either underlines or italics for titles of longer works, but don't mix the two styles in your project.

Notes

    1. Helen Wilkinson, "It's Just a Matter of Time," *Utne Reader* (May/June 1995): 66-67.

    2. Paul Osterman, "Getting Started," *Wilson Quarterly* (Autumn 1994): 46-55.

    3. James Morgan, "Blue Highways," in *The Distance to the Moon* (New York: Riverhead, 1999), 93.

    4. Ibid., 97.

    5. Wilkinson, 66.

    6. Ibid.

    7. Ibid., 67.

Notice that note 4 refers to the Morgan chapter, and notes 6 and 7 refer to Wilkinson's article.

b   Chicago Bibliographies

At the end of your project, list alphabetically every source cited or used in the paper. Title the list "Works Cited" if it includes only works actually mentioned in the essay; title it "Bibliography" if it also includes works consulted in preparing the project but not actually cited. Because Chicago notes are quite thorough, a Works Cited or Bibliography page may be optional; consult your instructor.

When an author has more than one work on the list, arrange them alphabetically under the author's name, using this form.

Altick, Richard D. *The Shows of London.* Cambridge: Belknap-Harvard University Press, 1978.

---. *Victorian People and Ideas.* New York: Norton, 1973.

---. *Victorian Studies in Scarlet.* New York: Norton, 1977.

Bibliographies: Chicago Style

- Center the title ("Works Cited" or "Bibliography") at the top of a new page after the end of your piece. Don't use quotation marks around the title.
- Single-space within each entry; double-space between entries.
- Arrange the list alphabetically by author's last name.
- Start each entry at the left margin; indent subsequent lines of an entry like a paragraph.

Works Cited

Frazer, R. M. *A Reading of "The Iliad."* Lanham, Md.: University Press of America, 1993.

Homer. *The Iliad.* Translated by Robert Fitzgerald. New York: Anchor Press, 1974.

Kirk, G. S. *"The Iliad": A Commentary.* Vol. 2. New York: Cambridge Univ. Press, 1990.

Toohey, Peter. "Epic and Rhetoric: Speech-making and Persuasion in Homer and Apollonius." *Arachnion: A Journal of Ancient Literature and History on the Web* 1 (1995). Journal online. Available from http://www.cisi.unito .it/arachne/num1/toohey.html; Internet; accessed 21 February 1996.

c Chicago Models

In this section, you will find the Chicago notes and bibliography forms for more than twenty types of sources. The numbered items in the list are the sample note forms, often showing the specific page numbers as you would when preparing actual notes; the matching bibliography entries appear immediately after.

92. Book, One Author—Chicago

1. Steven Weinberg, *Dreams of a Final Theory* (New York: Pantheon Books, 1992), 38.

Weinberg, Steven. *Dreams of a Final Theory.* New York: Pantheon Books, 1992.

93. Book, Two or Three Authors or Editors—Chicago

2. Peter Collier and David Horowitz, *Destructive Generation: Second Thoughts about the '60s* (New York: Summit, 1989), 24.

Collier, Peter, and David Horowitz. *Destructive Generation: Second Thoughts about the '60s.* New York: Summit, 1989.

94. Book, Edited—Focus on the Original Author—Chicago

3. William Shakespeare, *The Complete Works of Shakespeare,* 4th ed., ed. David Bevington (New York: Longman, 1997).

Shakespeare, William. *The Complete Works of Shakespeare.* 4th ed. Edited by David Bevington. New York: Longman, 1997.

95. Book Written by a Group—Chicago

4. Council of Biology Editors, *Scientific Style and Format: The CBE Manual for Authors, Editors, and Publishers,* 6th ed. (Cambridge: Cambridge Univ. Press, 1994).

Council of Biology Editors. *Scientific Style and Format: The CBE Manual for Authors, Editors, and Publishers.* 6th ed. Cambridge: Cambridge Univ. Press, 1994.

96. Book with No Author—Chicago List it by its title, excluding *The, A,* or *An.*

> 5. *Webster's Collegiate Thesaurus.*
> (Springfield: Merriam, 1976).

Webster's Collegiate Thesaurus. Springfield:
   Merriam, 1976.

97. Work of More Than One Volume—Chicago

> 6. Karlheinz Spindler, *Abstract Algebra
> with Applications* (New York: Dekker, 1994),
> 1:17–18.

Spindler, Karlheinz. *Abstract Algebra with
   Applications.* Vol. 1. New York: Dekker,
   1994.

98. Chapter in a Book—Chicago

> 7. Delia Owens and Mark Owens, "Home to
> the Dunes," in *The Eye of the Elephant: An
> Epic Adventure in the African Wilderness*
> (Boston: Houghton Mifflin, 1992), 11–27.

Owens, Delia, and Mark Owens. "Home to the
   Dunes," *In The Eye of the Elephant:
   An Epic Adventure in the African
   Wilderness.* Boston: Houghton Mifflin,
   1992.

99. Article in a Scholarly Journal—Chicago Scholarly journals are usually identified by volume number or season (rather than day, week, or month of publication). Such journals are usually paginated year by year, with a year's work treated as a volume. Provide author(s), title of the work (in quotation marks), name of periodical (underlined or italicized), volume number, date of publication, and page numbers.

> 8. Karl P. Wentersdorf, "Hamlet's
> Encounter with the Pirates," *Shakespeare
> Quarterly* 34 (1983): 434–48.

Wentersdorf, Karl P. "Hamlet's Encounter
   with the Pirates." *Shakespeare
   Quarterly* 34 (1983): 434–48.

100. Article in a Popular Magazine—Chicago

> 9. Don Graham, "Wayne's World," *Texas
> Monthly,* March 2000, 110–11.

Graham, Don. "Wayne's World." *Texas Monthly,*
   March 2000, 110–11.

When an article does not appear on consecutive pages omit page numbers in the bibliography entry.

101. Article or Selection from a Reader or Anthology—Chicago

10. Pamela Samuelson, "The Digital Rights War," in *The Presence of Others,* 3d ed., ed. Andrea Lunsford and John Ruszkiewicz (New York: St. Martin's, 2000), 315–20.

Samuelson, Pamela. "The Digital Rights War." In *The Presence of Others.* 3d ed., edited by Andrea Lunsford and John Ruszkiewicz. New York: St. Martin's, 2000.

102. Article in a Newspaper—Chicago   Identify the edition of the paper cited (*final edition, home edition, Western edition*), except when citing editorials or features that appear in all editions. Since an individual story may move in location from edition to edition, page numbers are not ordinarily provided. Section numbers are given for papers so divided. Individual news stories are usually not listed in a bibliography.

11. Celestine Bohlen, "A Stunned Venice Surveys the Ruins of a Beloved Hall," *New York Times,* 31 January 1995, national edition, sec. B.

103. WWW—Web Site—Chicago   Citations for online sources generally include as many of the following pieces of information as are available: author of the content, title of the page, title or owner of the site, URL, and date of access.

12. University of Georgia, "Points of Pride," University of Georgia, http://www.uga.edu/profile/pride.html (accessed October 30, 2003).

University of Georgia, "Points of Pride," University of Georgia, http://www.uga.edu/profile/pride.html.

104. Article from an Electronic Journal (Database)—Chicago

13. Sandra Yin, "Color Bind," *American Demographics,* 25, no. 7 (2003). Academic Search Premier, via Galileo, http://www.galileo.usg.edu.

Yin, Sandra. "Color Bind." *American Demographics* 25, no. 7 (2003): 22–26.

```
Academic Search Premier, via Galileo,
http://www.galileo.usg.edu.
```

d Sample Chicago Pages

For a sample Works Cited list, see page 130. For a sample list of notes, see page 129.

1. Title page

In numbering Chicago papers, count the title page as a page, but do not number it.

Sample Title Page

```
            THE UNIVERSITY OF TEXAS AT AUSTIN
              DIOMEDES AS HERO OF THE ILIAD
                  E 309—TOPICS IN WRITING
              DIVISION OF RHETORIC AND COMPOSITION
                              BY
                     JEREMY A. CORLEY
                     28 FEBRUARY 2005
```

On the page following the title page, repeat the title, but use capital and lowercase letters.

2. Footnotes

Here are the last several lines of a page, followed by footnotes.

Footnotes

```
relatively unimportant as an insult, even a public
one.⁴ A soldier's duty is to defend his homeland
and fight in its wars, and Achilles misses

    1. Homer, The Iliad, trans. Robert Fitzgerald
(New York: Anchor Press, 1974), 14.
    2. R. M. Frazer, A Reading of "The Iliad"
(Lanham, Md.: University Press of America,
1993), 12.
    3. Homer, 15.
    4. Frazer, 11.
```

14 CSE Style

"To spell out the obvious is often to call it into question."
—ERIC HOFFER, writer, philosopher, longshoreman

Disciplines that study the physical world—physics, chemistry, biology—are called the *natural sciences;* disciplines that examine (and produce) technologies are described as the *applied sciences.* Writing in these fields is specialized, and no survey of all forms of documentation can be provided here. For more information about writing in the following fields, we suggest that you consult one of the following style manuals. For guidelines to writing in other scientific disciplines, visit <http://owl.english.purdue. edu/handouts/research/r_docsources.html>.

- **Chemistry:** *The ACS Style Guide: A Manual for Authors and Editors,* 2nd edition (1998)—American Chemical Society
- **Geology:** *Suggestions to Authors of Reports of the United States Geological Survey,* 7th edition (1991)—U.S. Geological Survey
- **Mathematics:** *A Primer of Mathematical Writing* (1997)—American Mathematical Society
- **Physics:** *AIP Style Manual,* 4th edition (1990)—American Institute of Physics

A highly influential manual for scientific writing is *Scientific Style and Format: The CBE Manual for Authors, Editors, and Publishers* (6th edition, 1994). In this chapter we briefly describe one of the two major methods of documentation advocated in that manual: the citation-sequence system. Because the Council of Biology Editors (CBE) changed its name to the Council of Science Editors (CSE), you may see this system referred to as both CSE style (as we do in this chapter) and CBE style.

EXPRESS!

There are two basic steps in the citation-sequence system.

1. In the text, use a raised number (the preferred form) or a number in parentheses to indicate a citation.

   Oncologists[1] are aware of trends in cancer mortality[2].

```
Oncologists (1) are aware of trends in
cancer mortality (2).
```

2. On a References page, give the publication information for each numbered citation in numerical order.

```
1. Devesa SS, Silverman DT. Cancer incidence
   and mortality trends in the United
   States: 1935-74. J Natl Cancer Inst 1978;
   60:545-71.
2. Goodfield J. The siege of cancer. New
   York: Dell; 1978. 240 p.
```

a In-Text Citations

The in-text citation leads your reader to the References page, where complete publication information is listed.

1. More than one source in a single note

Separate the numbers by a hyphen if they are in sequence and by commas if they are out of sequence.

```
Cancer treatment[2-3] has changed over the
decades. But Rettig[4] shows that the politics
of cancer research remains constant.
```

2. Two or more citations to one source

If you cite a source again later in the paper, refer to it by its original number.

```
Great strides have occurred in
epidemiological methods[5] despite the
political problems in maintaining research
support and funding described by Rettig[4].
```

b The References Page

On a separate page at the end of the text of your paper, list the sources you used in the order they occurred. The list is *not* alphabetical: Source 1 in the paper is the first source listed on the References page; source 2 the second item, and so on. Here is a sample References page.

References

1. Devesa SS, Silverman DT. Cancer incidence and mortality trends in the United States: 1935-74. J Natl Cancer Inst 1978;60:545-71.

2. Goodfield J. The siege of cancer. New York: Dell; 1978. 240 p.

3. Loeb LA, Ernster VL, Warner KE, Abbotts J, Laszo J. Smoking and lung cancer: an overview. Cancer Res 1984;44:5940-58.

4. Rettig RA. Cancer crusade: the story of the National Cancer Act of 1971. Princeton: Princeton Univ Pr; 1977. 382 p.

5. Craddock VM. Nitrosamines and human cancer: proof of an association? Nature 1983 Dec 15:638.

c CSE Citation–Sequence Models

Here are typical References entries for major types of sources. There are so many variations on these basic entries, however, that you will certainly want to check the *CBE Manual* when you do a major CSE-style paper.

1. **Book: CSE Citation-Sequence Entry**

   A book entry includes the following basic information.

   - Number assigned to the source.
   - Name of author(s), last name first, followed by a period. Initials are used in place of full first or middle names. Commas ordinarily separate the names of multiple authors.
   - Title of work, followed by a period. Only the first word and any proper nouns in a title are capitalized. The title is not underlined.
   - Place of publication, followed by a colon.
   - Publisher, followed by a semicolon. Titles of presses can be abbreviated.
   - Date, followed by a period.
   - Number of pages, followed by a period.

Example:

```
2. Goodfield J. The siege of cancer. New York:
   Dell; 1978. 240 p.
```

2. **Scholarly Article: CSE Citation-Sequence Entry**

This form is used for scholarly journals in which the pagination is continuous throughout the year. Include the following basic information.

- Number assigned to the source.
- Name of author(s), last name first, followed by a period. Initials are used in place of full first or middle names. Commas ordinarily separate the names of multiple authors.
- Title of article, followed by a period. Only the first word and any proper nouns in a title are capitalized. The title does not appear between quotation marks.
- Name of the journal. All major words are capitalized, but the journal title is not underlined. A space (but no punctuation) separates the journal title from the date. Journal titles of more than one word can be abbreviated following the recommendations in *American National Standard Z39.5–1985: Abbreviations of Titles of Publications.*
- Year (and month for journals not continuously paginated; date for weekly journals), followed immediately by a semicolon.
- Volume number, followed by a colon, and the page numbers of the article. No spaces separate these items. A period follows the page numbers.

Example:

```
1. Devesa SS, Silverman DT. Cancer incidence
   and mortality trends in the United States:
   1935-74. J Natl Cancer Inst 1978;60:545-71.
```

3. **Article in a Popular Magazine: CSE Citation-Sequence Entry**

Include the following basic information.

- Number assigned to the source.
- Name of author(s), last name first, followed by a period. Initials are substituted for first names unless two authors mentioned in the paper have identical last names and first initials.
- Title of article, followed by a period. Only the first word and any proper nouns in a title are capitalized. The title

does not appear between quotation marks. (Where quotation marks are needed, CSE recommends British style. See *CBE Manual,* pp. 180–81.)

- Name of magazine, abbreviated. All major words are capitalized, but the journal titles is not underlined. A space (but no punctuation) separates the magazine title from the year and month.
- Year, month (abbreviated), and day (for a weekly magazine). The year is separated from the month by a space. A colon follows immediately after the date, followed by page numbers(s). The entry ends with a period.

Example:

```
7. Zinder ND. The genome initiative: how to
   spell 'human'. Sci Am 1990 July:128.
```

4. **Electronic Item**

   Include the basic information provided for a print document (author, title, publication information, page numbers) with the following additions.

   - Electronic medium, identified between brackets. For books and monographs, this information comes after the title [*monograph online*]; for periodicals, it follows the name of the journal [*serial online*].
   - Availability statement, following the publication information or page numbers.
   - Date of access, if helpful in identifying what version of an electronic text was consulted.

Example:

```
9. Dewitt R. Vagueness, semantics, and the lan-
   guage of thought. PSYCHE [serial online]
   1993 July;1(1). Available from: ftp.lib.
   ncsu.edu via the INTERNET. Accessed 1995
   Apr 26.
```

Final Paper: CSE Style

- CSE style normally requires a separate title page. The title of the essay can be centered about a third of the way from the top of the page, followed by the word *by* on a separate line and the writer's name, also on a separate line. Other information such as instructor's name, course title, and date can be included on the bottom third of the page.

- CSE style normally requires an abstract of about 250 words on a separate sheet immediately following the title page. The title "Abstract" is centered on the page.
- Double-space the body of a CSE paper. Avoid hyphenating words at the end of the line.
- Number pages consecutively in the upper right-hand corner, counting the title page as the first page.
- Take special care with figures and tables. They should be numbered in separate sequences. The *CSE Manual* includes an entire chapter on handling illustrative material.
- The References page follows the text of the CSE essay on a new page. Remember that the items on this page are *not* listed alphabetically. References pages can also be titled "Literature Cited" or "References Cited."
- All works listed on the References page should be cited at least once in the body of your paper.
- Entries on the References page are single-spaced, with a space left between the entries.

Sentence Revision

15 Clarity

"I'll play with it first and tell you what it is later."

—MILES DAVIS, jazz musician

Clear sentences make it easy for a careful reader to move along steadily without backtracking to puzzle about meaning. As Miles Davis suggests, though, the act of creating—whether in music or writing—may change your original intention, so you may go through several drafts before you can decide whether your ideas are stated clearly.

EXPRESS!

Bring your writing down to earth. Check your sentences to be sure you don't go too long without mentioning someone or something specific—people readers can visualize, objects they can imagine, situations they can grasp. Using specific, sensory details will help make your writing clearer.

a Make Your Subject Clear

Make it easy for your reader to see your subject. Ask yourself, "What is the key word or concept in the sentence?" Then see if you can make that key word the subject.

Make people or concrete things the subject.

NO PEOPLE IN SUBJECT

The excitement of doing original research has not been experienced by most first-year college students.

PEOPLE AS SUBJECT

Most first-year college students don't know the excitement of doing original research.

Replace abstract words and phrases.

ABSTRACT AND OVERLOADED SUBJECT

The inability of standardized tests, from IQ tests to SAT scores, to predict people's behavior poses a long-standing dilemma for social scientists.

PEOPLE AS SUBJECT

Social scientists have long wondered why standardized tests, from IQ tests to SAT scores, predict behavior so poorly.

b Use Vigorous Verbs

Read your draft sentence and focus on the action. Ask, "What's happening?" Whenever you can, express that action in a single, lively verb.

Replace *to be* verbs with more vigorous verbs. Forms of *be—am, is, are, was, were, being, been*—are not as interesting as verbs that do things.

OVERUSED *TO BE* VERBS

It **is** the tendency of adolescents **to be more concerned** about the opinion of others in their age group than they **are** about the values parents **are** trying to instill in them.

REPLACED WITH ACTION VERBS

Adolescents **crave** the approval of their peers and often **resist** their parents' values.

Adolescents **care** more about their friends' opinions than their parents' values.

Reduce the number of passive verbs. Subjects perform actions in active sentences; in passive sentences, subjects receive the action. Make the subject the actor of the sentence, not the receiver.

PASSIVE VERB REVISED

the unsophisticated travelers ignored

Frequently, local customs ~~were ignored by the unsophisticated travelers.~~

When the action itself is more important than who performed it, or when you don't know who performed an action, retain the passive. For example, scientific and technical writing that focuses on processes and research results often requires the passive.

Apical dominance in this rose species **was minimized** by daily pruning.

Replace cluttered verb phrases with single lively verbs. For example, change *give consideration to* to *consider, make acknowledgment of* to *acknowledge, puts the emphasis on* to *emphasizes.*

oppose   *doubt*

Some groups who ~~are in opposition to~~ the death penalty ~~be-~~
~~lieve that there is doubt about~~ its morality.

Malls ~~always manage to~~ irritate me when they ~~start to~~ display
Christmas paraphernalia immediately after Halloween.

c Balance Parallel Ideas

Put parallel ideas in parallel form. Sentences are easier to
read when closely related ideas within them also follow similar
patterns of language. Sentence elements that come in pairs or
triplets should follow the same form: a noun with another
noun, an adjective phrase with another adjective phrase, and
so on.

Check structures that come in pairs or triplets.   Have you
used the same forms for each item? If not, stack up the mis-
matched elements and revise any that don't fit the pattern.

NOT PARALLEL

The best doctors are **patient,**

thorough, and

have a lot of compassion.

PARALLEL WORDS

The best doctors are **patient, thorough,** and **compassionate.**

NOT PARALLEL

Praised by critics and
being embraced by common readers,
the novel became a best-seller.

PARALLEL PHRASES

Praised by critics, embraced by common readers, the novel
became a best-seller.

NOT PARALLEL

Interest rates might be tightened, or
we might increase prices.

PARALLEL CLAUSES

Interest rates might be tightened, or **prices might be
increased.**

Check items in a list for parallel structure.

PARALLEL

The school board's objectives are clear: **to hire** the best teachers, **to create** successful classrooms, **to serve** the needs of all families, and **to prepare** the students for their future careers.

Use parallelism in comparisons using *as* or *than*.

Parallelism is required in comparisons following *as* or *than*.

Smiling takes fewer muscles than ~~to frown.~~
(frowning)

The city council is as likely to adopt the measure as ~~vetoing~~ it.
(to veto)

Use parallelism with expressions such as *either . . . or* and *both . . . and.*

Correlatives require parallel structure. Other correlatives include *neither . . . nor, on the one hand . . . on the other hand, not only . . . but also.*

As Franklin once remarked, either **we hang together** or **we hang separately.**

d | Use Specific Details

Readers will understand your ideas more easily when you use specific, concrete details: *Harley* instead of *two-wheeled vehicle* or even *motorcycle.* Obviously, you sometimes have to use abstract words to explain ideas, but for a general audience, the more specific your details, the better your piece will read. When writing for specialists, you can be more abstract.

- Replace abstract nouns with concrete nouns where possible: *building* with *farmhouse* or *brownstone*, for example.
- Replace long nouns with their shorter verb counterparts. This revision usually requires rewriting the whole sentence.

SPECIFIC DETAILS

If we don't yet breed children for their SAT scores, there is a whole class of people . . . who coach their toddlers to get into the nursery schools that offer a fast track to Harvard.
—Barbara Ehrenreich, "The Economics of Cloning"

If the writer had used an abstract phrase such as "the selection of offspring for desirable traits" to replace her more concrete example, her prose would be more difficult, not to mention less interesting, to read.

State a general idea and then provide more and more specific details about it.

Toi Soldier was a magnificent black Arabian stallion, a sculpture in ebony, his eyes large and dark, his graceful head held high on an arched neck.

Use examples to illustrate general statements.

To be in love is merely to be in a state of perpetual anesthesia—to mistake an ordinary young man for a Greek god or an ordinary young woman for a goddess.
—H. L. Mencken, *Prejudices, First Series*

e | State Ideas Positively

DIFFICULT TO READ

Do we have the right **not to be victims** of crime?

CLEARER

Do we have the right **to be safe** from crime?

f | Chunk Your Writing

If you think readers will find a lengthy sentence hard to read, consider breaking it into shorter, more manageable ones—as the following example illustrates. To present unusually complex information, consider creating a bulleted or numbered list.

In support of this proposal, they cite the example of
~~Citing an instance in which~~ a 16-year-old student ~~was~~ working 48 hours a week at Burger King in order to pay for a new car ~~and~~ *while* simultaneously trying to attend high school full time. New York educators have recently proposed legislation that prohibits high school students from working more than 3 hours on a school night, ~~limits~~ *The proposed law would* the total time ~~they~~ *students* can work in a week to 20 hours when school is in session, and ~~fines~~ *would* employers who violate these regulations as much as $2,000.

If your information is numerical, a graph or chart may be most effective.

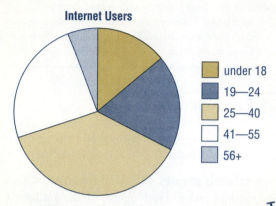

Internet Users

- under 18
- 19—24
- 25—40
- 41—55
- 56+

e-TIPS

"**C**hunk size" is crucial to the success of your Web page. Readers get more impatient with material online than they do with printed matter. Use more graphic organizers—bulleted and numbered lists, quick-loading charts and figures—than you might on the printed page. Keep your sentences short and lively, and your readers may linger at your site.

<DESTINATION>

For more strategies for improving sentence clarity, visit the Purdue University Online Writing Lab at <http://owl.english.purdue.edu/handouts/general/gl_sentclar.html>. ∎

16 Economy

"As to the Adjective: when in doubt, strike it out."

—Mark Twain, novelist and journalist

For those who aspire to be good writers, the war against what writer and editor William Zinsser calls "clutter" never ends. Such clutter consists of clichés, strung-out phrases, pointless repetitions, and overly detailed descriptions.

a Cut Extra Words

First drafts are often filled with clichés, strung-out phrases,
pointless repetitions, and dull abstractions. Prune them.

Replace sprawling phrases with single words.   Check to see
if prepositional phrases and verb phrases can be condensed.

~~In the modern society in which we live today,~~ M̂any people still
attend church regularly.

emphasizes
This book ~~puts an emphasis on~~ the social problems caused
by drug use.

Replace . . .	With . . .
in the event that	if
in light of the fact that	since
on the grounds that	because
regardless of the fact that	although
at this point in time	now
it is obvious that	obviously
on an everyday basis	routinely
is reflective of	reflects
has an understanding of	understands
is in opposition to	opposes

Cut needless redundancy.   Look for vague nouns as well as
paired expressions whose elements mean the same thing.

Our entire society has been corrupted by ~~the evil of~~ com-
mercialism.

The Apprentice ~~to me~~ is a reality TV ~~type of show.~~

Replace . . .	With . . .
her area of specialization	her specialty
round in shape	round
belonging and togetherness	belonging

easy and effortless	easy
ready and able	ready
proper and fitting	fitting
trim and slim	trim
willing and eager	willing

Cut surplus intensifiers.   Use intensifiers only when they add weight or power to your prose.

> The Grand Canyon is a ~~quite unique~~ geological treasure, ~~basically~~ formed by the relentless power of the Colorado River.

Replace . . .	**With . . .**
completely finished	finished
basically done	done
totally exhausted	exhausted
awful tragedy	tragedy
absolutely pointless	pointless

Cut nominalizations.   Nominalizations are nouns made by adding endings to verbs and adjectives: *connectivity* from *connect, initialization* from *initial.* Restore the more lively verb or adjective by rewriting the sentence.

> Since ... don't sell well
> ~~Given the poor salability of~~ some products, manufacturers
> offer
> often ~~have to make offerings of~~ rebates.

b   Cut *It is* and *There are* Sentence Openings

Using these expletives habitually will make your prose dull and amateurish.

> F
> ~~There were~~ five of us huddled in the basement.

> T
> ~~Even~~ though ~~it is~~ the oldest of auto manufacturers, Mercedes remains innovative.

c   Condense

Say more with less: Condense sentences into clauses, clauses into phrases or words.

Check for repeated elements that can be combined.

The Concours D'Elegance ~~is~~ an annual exhibit of classic cars ~~The cars exhibited~~ often include handsome old Hudsons, Nashes, and Corvettes.

~~The geneticists had become~~ dissatisfied with the administrator's dishonest reports of their work ~~They~~ published their *the geneticists* own findings in the journal *Cell.*

Check for phrases that don't add meaning.

Thanksgiving is a time for all of us to be together ~~for the simple purpose of~~ enjoying each other's company.

Check for *who, which,* and *that.*

Ms. Rudneva, ~~who was~~ a former editor, left the company when she had twins.

<DESTINATION>

For ten strategies to eliminate wordiness, visit the Purdue OWL at <http://owl.english.purdue.edu/handouts/general/gl_concise.html>. ■

---

17 Variety

"Words ought to be a little wild for they are the assaults of thought on the unthinking."
—JOHN MAYNARD KEYNES, economist

Sentences should convey readers easily from point to point with clarity and emphasis. Using a variety of sentence structures allows you to guide readers to understand what is most important and relevant.

EXPRESS!

Experiment with each sentence in your draft to find a word order that creates the effect you are seeking. For example, the balance and parallelism of this sentence create a rhythm that makes the idea memorable.

Injustice anywhere is a threat to justice everywhere.

—Martin Luther King, Jr.

In this sentence, notice how the accumulating phrases allow the reader to savor each detail.

The crater spread toward the horizon, shallow and barren, ringed by flows of volcanic ash, crumbly as a dry cake.

Read your revised draft aloud to check the clarity and rhythm of the piece overall.

a Combine Short Sentences

If your prose seems choppy, see if you can combine related sentences with coordinate or subordinate clauses. Combining short sentences will smooth out your prose and, often, make your ideas clearer.

Check for strings of simple sentences. When many sentences in a row consist of simple subject plus verb combinations, the effect is monotony. Combine sentences with a comma and the coordinating conjunction—*and, or, nor, for, but, yet,* and *so*—that best expresses the relationship between the sentences.

SAT scores in math rose nationally, *but* Verbal scores dropped.

Notice the placement of the comma *before* **but.**

You can also coordinate elements within sentences. Note that a comma *precedes* **and.**

Elizabeth Cruse is working on her résumé. ~~She is also~~ planning *and* her interview with New Horizons Enterprises. ~~She is~~ completing her master's degree in marketing.

The occasional short sentence, however, adds drama.

Jesus wept.

Subordinate some sentences. Link subordinate clauses to related independent clauses with words such as *because, until, since, although, before, when, where, if.*

when
Many people go into debt. ~~C~~redit is easy to get.

because
The film enjoyed a brisk summer box office. ~~I~~t won an Academy Award last March.

Because the film won an Academy Award last March, it enjoyed a brisk summer box office.

When a subordinate clause *precedes* the independent clause, use a comma to set it off.

Highlight the contrast between independent clauses. Use a semicolon and the conjunctive adverb—*however, moreover, therefore,* and so on—that best expresses the relationship.

Members of the zoning board appreciated the developer's
arguments. ⟨; *however,*⟩ They rejected her rezoning request.

When **however** comes between two independent clauses, a semicolon precedes it and a comma follows.

b Expand Simple Sentences with Interesting Details

Not all simple sentences are short; you can expand them by compounding or modifying their subjects (S), verbs (V), or objects (O).

	S	V	O
ORIGINAL SENTENCE	Bugs	scare	people.

EXPANDED S	Tiny spiders, harmless caterpillars, and frail mantises
EXPANDED V	terrify or even paralyze
EXPANDED O	full-grown adults, from Ph.D.'s in physics to NFL linebackers

REVISED SENTENCE

Tiny spiders, harmless caterpillars, and frail mantises sometimes terrify or even paralyze full-grown adults, from Ph.D.'s in physics to NFL linebackers.

Of course, you'll never want to expand simply to create a longer sentence. Your purpose for writing will likely determine whether adding details such as these makes the sentence more effective.

c | Vary Sentence Openings

Move a word, phrase, or clause to the beginning of a sentence to increase sentence variety.

Fortunately, our finances improved.

In the eyes of our children, we parents are gods.

To express their criticism of the political establishment, folkrock musicians of the 1960s wrote protest songs.

Occasionally, you may invert the usual word order to create special effects.

Gone are the days when our children could roam the neighborhood freely.

<DESTINATION>

For excellent discussion, examples, and exercises on improving sentence variety, visit "Avoiding Primer Language," "The Garden of Phrases," and "Sentence-Combining Skills" at Capital Community Technical College's Guide to Grammar and Writing at <http://www.ccc.commnet.edu/grammar/>. ∎

18 Consistency and Sentence Logic

"A place for everything, everything in its place."

—BENJAMIN FRANKLIN, writer, scientist, printer

Sentences must make sense. Verbs have to express actions or states of being that the subject is capable of performing or experiencing. Compound structures should be parallel in form, and comparisons must be completed logically. The reader should not be left wondering how the writer intended a sentence to be completed.

> ### EXPRESS!
>
> Consider how simple features of your word processor can help you find illogical or ungrammatical elements in your sentences. For example, save your draft in a new file specifically for sentence editing. To aid you in examining one sentence at a time, create a double space between each sentence. Within a sentence, boldface the subject and the main verb, and then check whether they make sense together. Check items that come in pairs or triplets by arranging the paired elements in a vertical column (see page 144). If you often misplace modifying words such as *only* or *even,* use the "Find" feature to locate each instance for checking. Use all the tools you possess to make sure your sentences make sense.

a Revise Sentence Elements So They Work Together

Logically, the subject must be able to perform the action of the verb, and similarly, words that relate to each other, such as subjects and their complements, must fit together grammatically.

Revise when the subject and predicate don't fit together.

Ellen's **pleasure** in gardening ~~yearned~~ for a bigger yard. *(made her yearn)*

Pleasure cannot *yearn;* only people can.

The **windows** of the boutique ~~concentrate~~ their~~~~ attention ~~on~~ suburban hip-hop wannabes. *(attract)* *(of)*

Windows cannot *concentrate.*

Revise to make objects and complements match the words to which they are attached.

FAULTY

The kinds of **trips** we love to take are **hunting** and **fishing.**

Hunting and *fishing,* used as nouns, are activities, not trips.

POSSIBLE REVISION

We love to take **hunting and fishing trips.**

FAULTY

These negative attitudes **intimidate** the **enthusiasm** of the volunteers.

Intimidate requires people as its object.

POSSIBLE REVISION

Negative attitudes **undermine** the **enthusiasm** of volunteers.

b   Revise the Pattern *something is when*

Common in speech, *something is when* is substandard in written work. Linking verbs, such as *is* and *are*, act like equations; they signal that the words on each side of the verb are the same kinds of words.

FAULTY

Plagiarism is when you use someone else's work without giving proper credit.

Plagiarism is a noun, so its definition must be another noun or noun equivalent.

POSSIBLE REVISION

Plagiarism is using someone else's work without giving proper credit.

Now *plagiarism* is defined by the noun clause that begins *using someone else's work.*

POSSIBLE REVISION

Plagiarism results when a writer fails to credit a source.

Here *plagiarism* is defined by using an active verb to show a process.

c   Revise Tangled Sentences

Sentences sometimes start off in one direction, but then, at a connecting place, seem to "derail" and go in a different direction.

A modifying clause or phrase can cause problems.

OFF TRACK

It is a fact that juveniles, when sent to adult prisons rather than juvenile facilities, two-thirds of them go on to commit more serious crimes.

Lift out the phrase *when sent to adult prisons rather than juvenile facilities* to see that the opening of the sentence doesn't connect with the ending: *It is a fact that juveniles two-thirds of them go on to commit more serious crimes.*

POSSIBLE REVISION

Two-thirds of juveniles, when sent to adult prisons rather than juvenile facilities, go on to commit more serious crimes.

A crucial sentence element may be missing.

INCOMPLETE

If a person is energetic and bright, expecting to do well at our firm.

Here, the opening subordinate clause must eventually connect with an independent clause, but the writer has not supplied one.

POSSIBLE REVISION

If a person is energetic and bright, he or she can expect to do well at our firm.

DERAILED

By writing an excellent legal thriller can make an author a best-seller.

By marks a prepositional phrase. Prepositional phrases cannot function as subjects.

POSSIBLE REVISION

By writing an exciting legal thriller, an author can make the best-seller list.

d Place Modifiers Carefully

Modifiers should be placed near the words they modify. Misplaced modifiers are too far away from the word they modify, causing confusion. Dangling modifiers don't have a word or phrase to modify at all.

Be sure that an introductory modifying phrase is followed directly by the word it modifies, usually the subject of the sentence.

Mirella is unconcerned about

Never having had children, rising college costs ~~do not concern~~ ~~Mirella.~~

Supply a word for a dangling modifier to modify.

LaTisha found that

On returning to the room, the furniture had been rearranged.

Place limiting modifiers such as *only*, *even*, *almost*, *nearly*, and *just* immediately before the word they modify.

> **MISPLACED**
>
> Much to his dismay, Hugo realized he had **almost** dated every woman at the party.
>
> Did he date any of the women?
>
> **CLARIFIED**
>
> Much to his dismay, Hugo realized he had dated **almost** every woman at the party.

When a sentence has more than one verb, make sure it is clear which one the adverb modifies.

> **MISPLACED**
>
> Hearing the guard's footsteps approach **quickly** Mark emptied the safe.
>
> Were the footsteps approaching quickly or did Mark empty the safe quickly?
>
> **CLARIFIED**
>
> Hearing the guard's footsteps approach, Mark **quickly** emptied the safe.
>
> Note that a comma also helps keep the ideas sorted.

e | Add Needed Words

Missing words can derail sentences. Make sure you supply all the words needed to make sentences complete and grammatical.

Add missing words to complete compound structures.

> *broken*
> I never have ∧ and never will break a promise I make to you.
> *to*
> It costs money both to apply ∧ and graduate from college.

Without the words added in revision, the sentences are not grammatically correct. Revised, the verb phrase *have broken* parallels the verb phrase *will break;* each consists of a helping verb followed by the appropriate form of the main verb. In the second sentence, *apply to* parallels *graduate from.* Each includes a verb followed by the appropriate preposition.

Add missing words to make comparisons logical.

> The programming on cable TV is better suited to young
> ___that of___
> people than ˄ the networks.

Two unlike things are compared in the original version: programming and networks.

> ___those of___
> Juan's responsibilities are greater than ˄ the other aides at the hospital.

Responsibilities is illogically compared to *workers*. Adding *those of* compares Juan's responsibilities to theirs.

Add the word *that* if needed to prevent misreading.

> ___that___
> Many observers doubt ˄ the state leaders in the House and Senate are in favor of stronger laws to protect women from abusive domestic partners.

The addition of *that* prevents the reader from thinking that the observers doubt the leaders.

PART FIVE

Sentence Grammar

19 Repair Sentence Fragments

"I was going to have cosmetic surgery until I noticed the doctor's office was full of portraits by Picasso."

—RITA RUDNER, comic

Sentence fragments are clauses or phrases that look like complete sentences, but either they lack subjects or verbs or they are subordinate constructions. A complete sentence requires at least one independent clause.

The bill died. **Because the President vetoed it.**

The word *because* changes the independent clause *The President vetoed it* into a subordinate clause, which cannot be presented as a separate sentence.

EXPRESS!

To make sure you catch the fragments in your draft, check every sentence.

1. Does it have a subject-verb pair, with no subordinating word before the pair?
2. Does a verb end in *-ing* or does it follow the word *to*? If so, check to be sure another verb in the sentence is acting as the main verb.
3. Are lists that start with phrases such as *for example* attached to the sentence that precedes them?

This brief check will help you identify many common sentence fragment errors.

To repair sentence fragments, (1) attach the fragment to a related sentence or (2) revise the fragment to make it a complete sentence on its own.

a Clause Fragments

Clause fragments can appear to be complete sentences because they have both a subject and a verb. However, the subordinate words that begin such clauses make them dependent on other ideas for completeness. Subordinating words include *although, because, if, since, unless, when,* and *while.* Words that begin relative clauses—such as *who, which, that,* and *where*—also signal clauses that must be attached to complete sentences.

                        if
It will be a miracle, ~~If~~ the mail comes on time.

                             the
When we arrived at the canyon. ~~The~~ sun had already risen.

                              w
Roberto was the son of immigrants, Who had never aspired to public office.

                           They
Roberto was the son of immigrants. ~~Who~~ had never aspired to public office.

b | Phrase Fragments

A phrase fragment lacks a subject, a complete verb, or both. Verbal phrases—phrases with gerunds, participles, or infinitives—are especially tricky because they look like verbs but act as nouns, adjectives, or adverbs. Remember,

- An *-ing* word by itself can never act as the verb of a sentence. It must have an auxiliary verb such as *have, is,* or *were.*
- An infinitive, such as *to run* or *to get,* can never act as the verb of a sentence.

VERBAL FRAGMENTS

Suspecting a coverup, the
~~The~~ reporter asked the senator probing questions. ~~Suspecting a coverup.~~

To create the special effects for *Star Wars.* Industrial Light and Magic was founded by director George Lucas.

An appositive phrase, a word or word group that explains another noun or pronoun, cannot stand alone as a sentence.

                        the
The Capitol is on Congress Avenue. ~~The~~ widest street in the city.

c | Fragments with Lists

Sometimes a list gets detached from the sentence that introduced or explained it. Lists are often introduced by words or phrases such as *especially, for instance, for example,* and *such as.* Often you can attach the list to the preceding sentence with a colon or a dash.

People suffer from many peculiar phobias. For example, ail-urophobia (fear of cats), aviophobia (fear of flying), and vestiphobia (fear of clothes).

—for ⌃

d | Intentional Fragments

Intentional fragments are groups of words that convey full ideas even though they may lack subjects, verbs, or both. Intentional fragments enable writers to set a quick pace, present a series of vivid images, or establish a casual tone; they are often used in creating dialogue. You may find intentional fragments in fiction, advertising, and popular magazines.

Man is the only animal that blushes. Or needs to.

—Mark Twain

So what's the best choice? Simple: the PowerCenter 150 from Power Computing.

In any formal or academic writing, fragments should not appear regularly. For readers conservative about grammar, avoid fragments entirely.

<DESTINATION>

To practice identifying and eliminating fragments, visit The Purdue University OWL at
<http://owl.english.purdue.edu/handouts/grammar/g_frag.html>. ■

20 Repair Run-on Sentences

"Never express yourself more clearly than you are able to think."

—Neils Bohr, physicist

A comma splice occurs when you try to join two indepen-dent clauses with only a comma. A run-on sentence results when no punctuation separates two independent clauses.

COMMA SPLICE

Shawna is an outstanding orator,_she has no formal training in speech.

RUN-ON

We were surprised by the package_quickly we tore it open.

These errors are serious because they blur the relationship between the independent clauses, but they are easy to identify and fix.

EXPRESS!

Note in each of the preceding examples two subject-verb pairs are present.

Shawna is, she has
We were   we tore

As you edit your sentences, search for subject-verb pairs to check whether each pair is separated from the other with a mark stronger than a comma. If only a comma separates them, revise your punctuation.

You have several options for fixing comma splices and run-on sentences.

a Separate Independent Clauses with a Period

Keiko carefully measured the chemicals for the experiment⊙She she made sure all weights were exact.

b Insert a Semicolon Between Independent Clauses

Use a semicolon when the clauses are closely related.

Marta's entire life revolves around ecological problems; she can speak of little else.

Donald was supposed to be on stage in five minutes; however, he was still putting on his costume.

Note that when a word such as *however* comes between independent clauses, a semicolon precedes it, and a comma follows it.

c Join Independent Clauses with a Comma and a Coordinating Conjunction

Coordinating conjunctions are *and, or, nor, for, but, yet,* and *so.*

His progress was slow because he did every step by hand, ^{*and*} it wasn't easy work.

d Subordinate One Clause to the Other

Albert had to finish the report by himself ^{*because*} his irresponsible co-author had lost interest in the cause.

‹DESTINATION›

To learn other strategies for identifying run-ons, visit the Writing Center at the University of North Carolina at Chapel Hill at <http://www.unc.edu/depts/wcweb/handouts/fragments.html>. ■

21 Make Subjects and Verbs Agree

"When I was young, I never wanted to leave the court until I got things exactly correct. My dream was to become a pro."
—LARRY BIRD, basketball player and coach

Verbs must agree with their subjects in person (*I, you, he, she,* or *it*) and number (singular or plural). With verbs in the present tense, agreement in number is simple: Most subjects take the base form of the verb.

I wait. We wait. You wait. They wait.

The exception to this pattern occurs with third-person singular subjects, such as *he, she, it, the plumber, Ms. Jones.* For these subjects, you must add *-s* or *-es* to the base form.

The plumber wait**s**. She wait**s**.

Ms. Jones go**es**. He go**es**.

EXPRESS!

You can find many subject-verb agreement errors by crossing out all the prepositional phrases in a sentence—for example, phrases beginning with *of, in,* and *at.* When you see what words remain, you may find it easier to identify the true subject of the sentence.

continues
Danger ~~of all types continue~~ to attract people.

You can also cross out all phrases that begin and end with a comma to find the true subject.

embrace
All politicians, ~~regardless of their ideology, embrace~~ the goal that every child should be able to read by the end of third grade.

These two simple steps will help you catch many typical agreement errors.

---

a   Words Between Subject and Verb

When subjects and verbs are separated by other word groups, make sure the verb agrees with the subject and not another noun that falls in between.

were
The numerous dams in the river ~~was~~ built by beavers.

Phrases such as *along with, as well as,* or *together with* do not make a singular subject plural.

The National Weather Service, as well as many police officers,
wishes
~~wish~~ amateurs wouldn't chase severe storms.

When a singular verb sounds awkward, consider joining the subjects with *and* instead.

---

b   Subjects Joined by *and*

Subjects joined by *and* are usually plural.

indicate
Hail and a rotating cloud wall ~~indicates~~ the possibility of a tornado.

Exceptions: Treat the compound subject as singular in the following cases.

- the two parts of the subject describe a single idea: *Peace and quiet **is** rare. Rock and roll **is** here to stay.*
- the subject is preceded by *every* or *each*: *Each spring and each fall **brings** the danger of more clouds. Every storm chaser and newsperson **wants** great pictures of the storm.*

c Subjects Joined by *or* or *nor*

The verb, or its auxiliary, agrees in number with the subject nearer to the verb.

Heavy rain or baseball-sized hail ~~cause~~ *causes* the most damage.

Either severe lightning or powerful bouts of hail ~~is~~ *are* apt to accompany the development of a supercell.

d Indefinite Pronouns Such as *anyone*

Indefinite pronouns are pronouns that do not refer to a particular person, thing, or group. In formal writing, treat the following indefinite pronouns as singular: *anybody, anyone, anything, everybody, everyone, everything, nobody, no one, nothing, somebody, someone, something, each.*

Each **believes** decisive action needs to be taken.

Some indefinite pronouns vary in whether they refer to an individual or a group: *all, any, either, more, most, neither, none, some.* Use the singular or plural depending on the meaning you intend.

Most of this apple **is** rotten.

Most of the voters **favor** the legislation.

Few, many, and *several* are always plural.

e Collective Nouns Such as *team*

Collective nouns name a group: *team, choir, band, orchestra, jury, committee, faculty, family.* Usually, collective nouns emphasize the group as a unit, and they take singular verbs. However, they sometimes refer to separate individuals or parts of the group, and in this case, they take plural verbs.

SINGULAR

The jury **expects** its verdict to be controversial.

PLURAL

The jury **agree** not to discuss their verdict with the press.

Usually your writing will be smoother if you treat collective nouns as singular subjects.

Note: Measurements are singular as a unit but plural as individual components.

Six months **is** the waiting period.

Six months **have** passed.

f | Subject After Verb

A verb agrees with its subject, no matter where the subject appears in the sentence.

Was their motive to get revenge?

Among those requesting Chief Harley's resignation **were** many citizens.

Here **is** a surprising turn of events.

g | *Who, which,* and *that* as Subjects

The relative pronouns *who, which,* and *that* refer to antecedents, just as other pronouns do. When a relative pronoun is used as a subject, the verb agrees with the antecedent.

The killer whale is a mammal that **demonstrates** highly complex social behavior.

A subtle agreement problem occurs with the phrase *one of the.* In general, use a plural verb form with *one of the,* but use a singular verb form when you add *only* to the phrase: *only one of the.*

seem

Ransom is one of the city officials who always ~~seems~~ enthusiastic.

Some officials always seem enthusiastic, and Ransom is one of them. *Who* refers to *city officials,* and the verb is plural.

                                                              seems
Ransom is the only one of the city officials who always ~~seem~~
enthusiastic.

Only one city official always seems enthusiastic—Ransom. *Who*
refers to *one,* and the verb is singular.

h Linking Verbs and Complements

Common linking verbs are *to be, to seem, to appear, to feel, to
taste, to look,* and *to become.* A linking verb agrees with its subject,
which usually precedes the verb, not with the subject complement, which follows it.

                                                       is
The key to a candidate's success ~~are~~ television appearances.

The subject is *key,* not *appearances.*

i Plural Forms, Singular Meanings

Some words that end in *-s* are singular in meaning and take
singular verbs: *physics, statistics, mathematics, measles, mumps,
news.* Consult a dictionary if you are unsure whether a word is singular or plural.

                    is
Mathematics ~~are~~ perceived as a difficult subject by many
students.

Other singular terms—*series, segment, portion, fragment,
part*—usually remain singular even when modified by plural
words.

                          is
A series of questions ~~are~~ posed by a reporter.

The word *majority* can function as both a singular and a
plural noun.

SINGULAR   The majority **rules.**

PLURAL   The majority of critics **want** the police chief to be
            fired.

j | Titles and Words Used as Words

Titles and words referred to as words always take singular verbs, even when their own forms are plural.

The Adventures of Rocky and Bullwinkle ~~star~~ *stars* Rene Russo as Natasha Fatale and Jason Alexander as Boris Badenov.

The word *physics* ~~come~~ *comes* from the Latin "physica," meaning "natural science."

<DESTINATION>

For a basic review of subjects and predicates, check out the guidelines from the University of Nevada Las Vegas Writing Center at <http://www.unlv.edu/Writing_Center/Subject-Verb%20Agreement.htm>. ■

22 | Check Verbs

"Any activity becomes creative when the doer cares about doing it right, or doing it better."
—JOHN UPDIKE, novelist

Verbs express actions and states of being: *run, exist.* They express the time or time frame in which actions occur—the past, present, future—and relations among events that happen at different times. Verbs also vary in form: Not all verbs form the past tense or past participles in a regular, consistent way. Verbs show whether a writer intends to make a statement, a command, or, more subtly, a wish, a hope, or a suggestion. Using the correct verb form requires close attention.

EXPRESS!

When editing verbs, first check an entire passage—a paragraph or group of related paragraphs—to discover whether you have established a dominant time frame for the passage. Do most of the verbs express current actions, for example? If not, read the passage carefully

(continued)

to decide on your main purpose. Are you describing something you want your readers to feel is happening now? If so, consider changing many of the verbs to the present tense. Are you recounting a past incident? Are you speculating about the future? Not all verbs have to be in a single tense. But unless you establish a dominant time frame, you are likely to confuse your readers.

a Regular and Irregular Verbs

Regular verbs form both the past tense and the past participle by adding *-d* or *-ed* to the base form of the verb: *advertise, advertised, advertised; talk, talked, talked*. Irregular verbs do not follow this pattern, however; they change their forms in various ways.

Consult a dictionary or the following list to be sure you're using the correct verb form. The list gives the three principal parts of each verb: the base form, or present tense; the simple past tense; and the past participle. The past participle is used with auxiliary verbs to form verb phrases such as *I have ridden, I had ridden, I will have ridden*.

Irregular verbs

Present	Past	Past Participle
arise	arose	arisen
bear (carry)	bore	borne
bear (give birth)	bore	borne, born
become	became	become
begin	began	begun
bite	bit	bitten, bit
blow	blew	blown
break	broke	broken
bring	brought	brought
burst	burst	burst
buy	bought	bought
catch	caught	caught
choose	chose	chosen
cling	clung	clung
come	came	come
creep	crept	crept
dig	dug	dug

Present	Past	Past Participle
dive	dived, dove	dived
do	did	done
draw	drew	drawn
dream	dreamed, dreamt	dreamed, dreamt
drink	drank	drunk
drive	drove	driven
eat	ate	eaten
fall	fell	fallen
find	found	found
fly	flew	flown
forget	forgot	forgotten
forgive	forgave	forgiven
freeze	froze	frozen
get	got	got, gotten
give	gave	given
go	went	gone
grow	grew	grown
hang (an object)	hung	hung
hang (a person)	hanged, hung	hanged, hung
know	knew	known
lay (to place)	laid	laid
lead	led	led
leave	left	left
lend	lent	lent
lie (to recline)	lay	lain
light	lit, lighted	lit, lighted
lose	lost	lost
pay	paid	paid
plead	pleaded, pled	pleaded, pled
prove	proved	proved, proven
ride	rode	ridden
ring	rang, rung	rung
rise	rose	risen
run	ran	run
say	said	said
see	saw	seen
set	set	set
shake	shook	shaken
shine	shone, shined	shone, shined
show	showed	shown, showed

(*continued*)

Irregular verbs (continued)

Present	Past	Past Participle
shrink	shrank, shrunk	shrunk
sing	sang, sung	sung
sink	sank, sunk	sunk
sit	sat	sat
speak	spoke	spoken
spring	sprang, sprung	sprung
stand	stood	stood
steal	stole	stolen
sting	stung	stung
swear	swore	sworn
swim	swam	swum
swing	swung	swung
take	took	taken
tear	tore	torn
throw	threw	thrown
wake	woke, waked	woken, waked
wear	wore	worn
wring	wrung	wrung
write	wrote	written

b *Lie* and *lay, sit* and *set, rise* and *raise*

These three pairs of verbs cause much confusion. *Lay, set,* and *raise* are all transitive verbs—they take direct objects. *Lay* means to "to place" or "to put"; *set* also means "to place" or "to put"; *raise* means "to lift up." These verbs require direct objects to complete their meanings.

Jenny **lays** a book on her desk. (*book* is the direct object)

Then she **sets** her plate on the nearby table. (*plate* is the direct object)

All this so her mother won't **raise** her voice in protest. (*voice* is the direct object)

Lie, sit, and *rise* are intransitive; they don't take objects. *Lie* means "to recline"; *sit* means "to take a seat"; and *rise* means "to get up."

Travis **lies** under the cottonwood tree.

He **sits** near the fountain to avoid the shade.

Then he **rises** and walks slowly away.

Consult this table to be sure you use the correct forms of these troublesome verbs.

Base Form	Present -s Form	Past	Present Participle	Past Participle
lie (recline)	lies	lay	lying	lain
lay (put)	lays	laid	laying	laid
sit (be seated)	sits	sat	sitting	sat
set (put)	sets	set	setting	set
rise (get up)	rises	rose	rising	risen
raise (lift)	raises	raised	raising	raised

c | Verb Tenses

Verb tense reveals when an action is taking place. English has three simple tenses; the present, past, and future. The present tense is used for actions occurring in the present and for actions that occur regularly. The past tense describes actions completed in the past. The future tense describes actions that will occur in the future.

PRESENT   I **answer** the question. I always answer.

PAST   I **answered** quickly.

FUTURE   I **will answer** the phone tomorrow.

The perfect forms of each tense (a form of *have* + the past participle) describe actions that were or will be completed by the time of another action.

PRESENT PERFECT   I **have answered** that question before.

PAST PERFECT   I **had answered** just before the alarm sounded.

FUTURE PERFECT   I **will have answered** the questions by Monday.

The progressive forms of each tense (a form of *be* + the present participle) express continuing actions.

PRESENT PROGRESSIVE	I **am answering** now.
PAST PROGRESSIVE	I **was answering** when the lights went out.
FUTURE PROGRESSIVE	I **will be answering** the phones all day.

The perfect progressive forms of each tense (a form of *have* + a form of *be* + the present participle) combine to express more complex time relationships.

PRESENT PERFECT PROGRESSIVE	I **have been answering** your questions.
PAST PERFECT PROGRESSIVE	I **had been answering** before you interrupted.
FUTURE PERFECT PROGRESSIVE	I **will have been answering** for nine hours by the time you arrive at midnight.

Use present tense for special purposes. Use the present tense to introduce quotations and refer to actions in literary works.

The doctor in *Macbeth* ~~warned~~ *warns* a gentlewoman, "You know what you should not" (5.1.46–47).

Use the present tense to express a general statement of fact or a scientific truth.

Einstein ~~argued~~ *argues* that the principle of relativity ~~applied~~ *applies* to all physical phenomena.

Use past perfect tense appropriately. The past perfect tense allows you to show exactly how one event in the past stands in relation to another event in time. Use it to make your writing more precise.

Tyneshia could not believe that Kyle *had* actually asked her to pay for his lunch.

Be consistent. Establish a dominant time frame in your writing and stick with it. Don't shift tenses needlessly; use different tenses to indicate shifts in time.

The lawyer had already explained the options to her client and was waiting for his decision.

<DESTINATION>

For more examples of using tense shifts appropriately, and for practice in revising unnecessary tense shifts, visit the Online Writing Lab at Purdue University at
<http://owl.english.purdue.edu/handouts/grammar/g_tensec.html>. ■

d Active and Passive Voice

Verbs that take objects (transitive verbs) can be in the active or passive voice. Voice indicates whether the subject of a sentence acts or is acted upon. In active voice, subjects perform actions; in passive voice, the action is done *to* the subject.

ACTIVE   Mr. Yeh **managed** the advertising campaign.

PASSIVE   The advertising campaign **was managed** by Mr. Yeh.

Many writers prefer active sentences because they are simple, direct, and easy to read; they keep prose lively. If you want to change a sentence from passive voice to active voice, make the performer of the action the subject of the sentence or clause.

Management approved the *the engineering staff completed*
~~The~~ designs ~~were approved by management~~ before work on them ~~was completed by the engineering staff.~~

Not every passive verb should be made active. The passive voice is useful, for example, when the action is more important than who performed it, or when you simply don't know who performed an action.

Dozens were arrested at the concert.

The van was stolen.

<DESTINATION>

Science, medical, and legal fields use the passive voice regularly; for a complete explanation of how to change a sentence from active to passive voice, visit "Guide to Grammar & Writing" at <http://webster.commnet.edu/grammar/passive.htm>. ■

e The Subjunctive Mood

Mood indicates how a writer intends a statement to be taken. If the writer is making a direct statement or asking a question, the mood is indicative. If the writer gives a command, the mood is imperative. The subjunctive mood is a bit more subtle. It is used to express a wish or a hope, make a suggestion, or speculate about how a situation might be. In most cases, you need only change a *was* to a *were* to mark the subjunctive mood.

> If Jimail ~~was~~ *were* in charge, we would be in good hands.

> If she ~~was~~ *were* to accept their terms, she could sign the contract.

Notice that the subjunctive verb is in the *if* clause, and the modal auxiliaries *would* and *could* are in the other clause.

For all verbs, the present subjunctive is the base form of the verb—*be, give, bless.* This is true even in the third-person singular, where you might expect a different form.

> The officer asked that everyone ~~is~~ *be* silent.

> It is essential that Emily ~~has~~ *have* her lines memorized by tomorrow.

For all verbs except *be,* the past subjunctive is the same as the simple past tense—*gave, blessed, sent.* For *be,* the past subjunctive is always *were.*

23 Check Pronouns

"You'll always miss 100% of the shots you don't take."
    —WAYNE GRETSKY, hockey player

Pronouns stand in for nouns and act like nouns, but they don't name a specific person, place, or thing—*I, you, he, she, it, we, they, whom, this, that, one,* and *which,* for example. A pronoun should clearly refer to its noun to avoid confusion (pronoun reference). A pronoun should match its noun in person, number, and gender (pronoun agreement). A pronoun's form should match its function in a sentence (pronoun case).

> *Workers* denied that **they** intended to strike.

The pronoun *they* clearly refers back to its noun, *workers.* The pronoun also agrees with the noun: Both are plural in number and subjective in case.

EXPRESS!

Pronouns alter the distance between you and your readers. Choosing *I, we,* or *you* puts you closer to readers; using *one* creates more distance. Take responsibility with *I* or *we,* speak directly to readers with *you,* and consider using *one* to convey a general truth or moral sentiment. Whether your writing situation calls for familiarity or distance, don't switch pronoun forms in the middle of a sentence or paragraph. Maintain a reasonable consistency for your readers' sake.

---

a Pronoun Reference

The noun a pronoun refers to is called its *antecedent.* The antecedent is the word you'd have to repeat in a sentence if you couldn't use a pronoun—*workers* in the previous example.

Revise ambiguous references. When a pronoun could refer to two possible antecedents, revise the sentence.

> When ~~Jackie talked to Andrea that~~ noon, ~~she~~ did not realize
> *they talked* ... *at Jackie*
>
> that ~~she~~ might be resigning before the end of the day.
> *Andrea*

Because both Jackie and Andrea are female, the pronoun *she* in the original sentence could refer to either of them.

Check *this, that, which,* and *it*. Pronouns must refer to specific antecedents. Pronouns can't refer to a group of words or to a vague idea. Replace the pronoun with a noun, add a specific antecedent, or change other wording to make your reference clear.

> The novel is filled with violence, brutality, and refined language. I especially like this *combination of toughness and grace.*

> The house has a tiny kitchen and a dilapidated porch ~~which the owners intend to remodel.~~ *, which the owners intend to remodel,*

nuclear power

While nuclear waste products are hard to dispose of safely, ~~it~~ remains a reasonable alternative to burning fossil fuels to produce electricity.

Check to be sure the antecedent is stated. Pronouns can't refer to antecedents that are merely implied in the sentence. Be especially careful to check for a stated antecedent when the pronoun is *they* or *it*.

people

In Houston, ~~they~~ live more casually than in Dallas.

The

~~In the~~ paper, ~~it~~ said that we should pass new school bonds.

Make sure the antecedent is not a possessive form. Possessive nouns—such as *expert's, children's, Smiths'*—cannot be used as antecedents.

experts   *the Miata*

As for the ~~experts' view of the Miata,~~ they either praise ~~it~~ or wish it had more power.

<DESTINATION>

For more discussion and examples of pronoun reference, as well as practices, visit *HyperGrammar* at the University of Ottawa at <http://www.uottawa.ca/academic/arts/writcent/hypergrammar/pronref.html>. ■

b Pronoun Agreement

Pronouns and nouns are either singular or plural. Make sure the pronoun matches the noun: Singular pronouns go with singular nouns, and plural pronouns go with plural nouns.

A victorious quarterback always enjoys hearing hometown crowds cheering in the stands for ~~them.~~ *him*

Check pronouns that refer to collective nouns. Collective nouns describe groups or collections of things: *class, team, band, orchestra, jury, committee, audience, family, Congress.* Usually, collective nouns refer to a group as a single unit, so pronouns that refer to collective nouns are usually singular. If you use a collective noun to refer to individual members of a group, however, then the noun is plural and the pronoun must also be plural.

its
The jury rendered ~~their~~ decision.

their
The chorus took ~~its~~ seats.

In most cases, sentences sound more natural if you treat collective nouns as singular. You can always add the word *members* before a collective noun when you are referring to individuals. *Members* becomes the antecedent, and the pronoun is plural.

The *members* of the chorus took **their** seats.

Check pronouns that refer to indefinite pronouns. First, decide whether an indefinite pronoun is singular or plural.

ALWAYS SINGULAR

anybody, anyone, anything, each, everybody, everyone, everything, nobody, no one, nothing, somebody, someone, something

ALWAYS PLURAL

few, many, several

Then make sure the pronoun matches the indefinite pronoun in number.

his or her
Everyone is entitled to ~~their~~ opinion.

his or her
Each of the legislators had ~~their~~ say.

Some indefinite pronouns can be either singular or plural, depending on how you use them. These pronouns are *all, any, either, more, most, neither, none,* and *some.* Sometimes, words modifying the pronoun may determine the number.

All of the portraits had yellowed in **their** frames.

All of the wine is still in **its** casks.

None is considered variable because it is often accepted as a plural form. However, in formal writing, *none* is usually treated as singular.

None of the churches had **its** doors locked.

Check antecedents joined by *or* and *nor*. When two singular antecedents are joined by *or, nor, either . . . or,* or *neither . . . nor,* refer to them with a singular pronoun.

its
Neither Brazil nor Mexico will raise ~~their~~ oil prices today.

When two plural antecedents are joined by these words, use plural pronouns to refer to them.

Either the players or the managers will file **their** grievances.

When a singular noun is joined to a plural noun by these words, the pronoun should agree with the nearer noun in number and in gender.

Either the stress-filled hours in the office or a poor diet will take ~~their~~ *its* toll on the business executive.

<DESTINATION>

For detailed examples of how to correct basic problems of pronoun agreement, visit The Write Place at St. Cloud State University at <http://leo.stcloudstate.edu/grammar/pronante.html>.

c | Pronoun Case

The personal pronouns and the pronoun *who* change in form—or case—according to their function in a sentence. Pronouns used as subjects or subject complements take the subjective case; pronouns used as objects take the objective case; and pronouns used as possessives take the possessive case.

Subjective Case	Objective Case	Possessive Case
I	me	my, mine
we	us	our, ours
you	you	your, yours
he	him	his
she	her	her, hers
it	it	its, of it
they	them	their, theirs
who	whom	whose

In most cases, writers automatically select the right form. But in a few situations, choosing between *I* and *me, he* or *him,* or *who* and *whom* can be tricky.

<DESTINATION>

To review pronoun case, visit Purdue University Online Writing Lab at <http://owl.english.purdue.edu/handouts/grammar/g_proncase.html>.

Check pairs of pronouns. The second pronoun in a pair is often troublesome. If you take out the first pronoun, you'll often be able to tell immediately which case to use for the second one. Similarly, in a noun-pronoun pair, take out the noun and examine what's left.

> You and ~~me~~ don't have the latest designs yet. *(I)*

You would never say "Me don't."

> The memo praised you and ~~she~~. *(her)*

You wouldn't say "praised she."

> The flowers are for Elena and ~~I~~. *(me)*

"For I"?

Check pronouns after linking verbs. Linking verbs, such as *to be, to seem, to appear, to feel,* and *to become,* connect a subject to a word or phrase that completes or extends its meaning—the subject complement. In formal writing, use the subjective case for the subject complement.

> It is ~~me~~. *(I)*

> You are ~~whom~~? *(who)*

> The next CEO will be ~~her~~. *(she)*

Check *we* or *us* when they are followed by nouns. The pronoun and following noun must share the same case. Take away the noun to check the case of the pronoun.

> ~~Us~~ lucky sailors missed the storm. *(We)*

"Us missed"?

> For ~~we~~ engineers, the job market looks promising. *(us)*

"For we"?

Check pronouns in comparisons. To determine pronoun case after *than, like,* or *as,* complete the comparison.

> I am taller than ~~him~~. *(he)*

I am taller than him is?

> We don't invest as much as ~~her~~. *(she)*

We don't invest as much as her does?

When the comparison could be completed either way, the pronoun you select will determine the meaning of the sentence. To avoid possible confusion, you can always write out the full comparison.

> Rodeos do not interest me as much as **she.** (as much as she interests me)

> Rodeos do not interest me as much as **her.** (as much as they interest her)

Check *who* and *whom*. The subjective form—*who* or *whoever*—is used when a pronoun is a subject or a subject complement. The objective form—*whom* or *whomever*—is used when a pronoun is an object.

> *Who*
> ~~Whom~~ wrote this letter?

Who is the subject.

> *whom*
> You addressed ~~who~~?

Whom is the object of the verb *addressed.*

> *whom*
> To ~~who~~ did you write?

Whom is the object of the preposition *to.*

When the pronoun is part of a subordinate clause, isolate the clause. Decide which case to use based on the pronoun's function in the clause, not in the whole sentence.

> ┌─ **subordinate clause** ─┐
> The system rewards whoever works hard.

Whoever is the subject of the clause *whoever works hard.* It has its own verb, *works.* Thus it is in the subjective case.

> ┌─ **subordinate clause** ─┐
> Juanita told her parents she would marry whomever she wanted.

In the clause *whomever she wanted,* the subject is *she,* the verb is *wanted,* and the object is *whomever.*

Check pronouns in appositives. Appositives are nouns or phrases that restate or add information to a previous noun. When an appositive contains a pronoun, the pronoun should be in the same case as the noun it modifies.

> *me*
> The instructor called two students, Sara and ~~I~~, to her office.

Two students, the noun phrase being modified, is the object of the verb *called.* So the pronoun should be in the objective case.

d | Nonsexist Pronoun Use

What should you do when you need to use a pronoun but don't know whether it should refer to a man or a woman?

Each of the editors walked to (his? her?) car.

Until a few years ago, most writers would use a masculine pronoun (*he, him, his*) in such a situation. However, this usage is sexist, because it implies that a particular group (of editors, pilots, engineers, senators, or students, for example) would not include any women. Similarly, in the following sentence, the implication is that only women are nurses.

SEXIST   An experienced nurse knows when **her** patient
needs extra care.

Clearly, even if this were true before, it is not true today—truck drivers, teachers, students, and secretaries can be men or women. Be sure that your language accommodates both sexes. (Obviously, you should acknowledge the inevitable exceptions: *Each of the nuns received an award for **her** assistance.*)

Use the expressions *he or she, him or her,* or *his or her.*

his or her spouse
Every secretary may invite ~~her husband.~~

However, *he* or *she* expressions quickly become tiresome. If you have more than one such expression in a sentence, consider your other choices.

Change a singular reference to a plural one.

leaving   all   s
Before ~~he or she leaves,~~ ~~each~~ member of the band should be
they   have   their
sure ~~he or she has his or her~~ music.

Delete the pronoun altogether.

without signing
Nobody should leave ~~until he has signed~~ the guest book.

For some readers, use a plural pronoun with indefinite pronouns formerly considered singular. Although this pronoun-referent *dis*agreement—very common in speech—is gaining limited acceptance in writing, be warned that many readers still consider such forms simply wrong.

their
Every skier took ~~his~~ turn on the ski slopes.

If you keep searching for the best way to make your language inclusive, you'll often find an excellent solution.

a
Every skier took ~~his~~ turn on the ski slopes.

Note that expressions such as *he/she, s/he,* and *s'he* are not widely accepted.

e Other Pronoun Problems

Two other problems writers sometimes have with pronouns are deciding when to use an apostrophe in the word *its* and knowing when to use *that, which,* and *who* in modifiers.

Its/it's and whose/who's. It is easy to confuse the possessive pronoun *its,* which has no apostrophe, with the contraction for *it is*—*it's*—which does include an apostrophe. The possessive forms of a personal pronoun never take an apostrophe, whereas contractions always require one.

its
The van lost ~~it's~~ hubcaps while parked on the street.

It's
~~Its~~ a shame that thefts in the neighborhood have increased.

If you consistently misuse *its/it's,* try reading *it's* as *it is* when checking your work. Eventually you will eliminate this error.

Similarly, *whose* is a possessive pronoun; *who's* is the contraction for *who is* or *who was.*

Whose
~~Who's~~ teammate is on first base?

Who's
~~Whose~~ on first?

That, which, and who. These words require special attention when they serve as relative pronouns introducing modifying clauses. Restrictive (essential) clauses are essential to understanding the terms they modify or explain. Restrictive clauses are not enclosed by commas and are often introduced by *that.*

The report ***that*** *I wrote* recommended the sale.

In contrast, the information in a nonrestrictive clause is important, but not essential to the meaning of the sentence. When a nonrestrictive clause is deleted, the sentence still makes sense. Nonrestrictive clauses are enclosed by commas and introduced by *which.*

The report, ***which*** *the team dashed off at the last minute,* recommended profit sharing.

Try removing the modifying clauses beginning with *that, which,* or *who.* Does the sentence still make sense, or will the reader be left with further questions? If the sentence still makes sense without the clause, then the clause is probably nonrestrictive and is enclosed by commas. If essential meaning is lost without the clause, then it is restrictive and is not enclosed by commas.

The popularity ***that*** *Charlie Chaplin enjoyed* during the early days of film may never be equaled.

Without the modifying clause, the sentence reads: *The popularity during the early days of film may never be equaled.* Essential meaning is lost; thus, the clause is restrictive and is not enclosed by commas.

His graceful gestures and matchless acrobatics, ***which*** *some critics likened to ballet,* were perfectly suited to the silent screen.

Without the modifying clause, the sentence reads: *His graceful gestures and matchless acrobatics were perfectly suited to the silent screen.* While the clause adds interesting additional detail, it is not essential to the main thought. Thus, the clause is nonrestrictive and is enclosed by commas.

The meaning you intend will often determine whether a modifying clause should be enclosed by commas.

The car **that** hit me rolled into the ditch.

Because no commas are used around *that hit me,* the sentence implies that several cars are involved, and the one that hit the writer, not one of the others, is the one that rolled into the ditch.

The car, **which** hit me, rolled into the ditch.

Now there's only one car, one that readers already know about. That it hit the writer is incidental information in a larger discussion about the car.

Finally, always use *who* rather than *that* or *which* to refer to a human subject:

The woman ~~that~~ waved was my boss.
who

24 Check Adjectives and Adverbs

"Never be afraid to sit awhile and think."
—LORRAINE HANSBERRY, playwright

Adjectives and adverbs carry important information, giving your reader specific details about other words in the sentence. Using the standard forms of adjectives and adverbs lends you credibility as a writer.

If you need help in placing adjectives, adverbs, and other modifiers, see 18d.

EXPRESS!

Add interest to your writing by varying your use of modifiers—adjectives, adverbs, phrases, and clauses. Consider how you can add layers of detail so that readers will not only understand your point but also enjoy reading about it. For example, in the following sentence, notice how the writer uses a variety of strategies to describe his subject.

Farmer is an inch or two over six feet and thin, unusually long-legged and long-armed, and he has an agile way of folding himself into a chair and arranging himself around a patient he is examining that made me think of a grasshopper.
—Tracy Kidder, "The Good Doctor"

a Adjectives

Adjectives modify nouns or pronouns; they answer the questions *which? how many?* and *what kind?*

Check for adjective pileups. Most, but not all, adjectives come before the nouns or pronouns they modify. You can add variety and interest by placing some adjectives after the words they modify. Revise your sentence when so many adjectives are strung together that readers will become confused or bored.

CONFUSING Adam had his ~~enthusiastic~~ *enthusiastic* parents' support.

TEDIOUS Our confident, ~~stylish, and experienced~~ *, stylish and experienced,* marching band won a national title.

Check words after linking verbs. Use adjectives—not adverbs—after linking verbs such as *seem, become, look, appear, feel,* and *smell.* These predicate adjectives give information about the subject of the sentence; they modify a noun or pronoun.

I feel bad~~ly~~.

Lillian acts optimistic~~ally~~ about her chances for getting into the graduate program.

Remember that some verbs can be used as both linking verbs and action verbs. If the verb describes an action rather than a state of being, use an adverb to modify the verb.

Wet dogs smell bad~~ly~~. (adjective after linking verb)

The dog smells rotting leaves excited*ly*. (adverb after action verb)

Check *good* and *well*. *Good* is always an adjective. Use *good* after a linking verb when you want to give information about the subject.

Jasper Hayes looks **good.**

When you are referring to someone's health, use *well* after the linking verb.

Most college students feel **well** in spite of their poor eating habits.

Don't use *good* as an adverb. Use *well* to modify verbs.

Most jobs in child care don't pay **well.**

Don't qualify absolute adjectives. Some adjectives express an absolute, something that cannot be compared or modified: *perfect, unique, singular, empty, equal, absolute, pregnant.* Don't use qualifiers (such as *less, more, most, least, very*) with these absolute adjectives.

Jack's story is ~~more~~ unique ~~than~~ Jane's.   *; is not*

Janice thought the software program was ~~absolutely~~ perfect.

<DESTINATION>

Nonnative speakers may find helpful the pages on "Grammar When You Need It," "Position of Adjectives," and, especially, "Order of Adjectives" at
<http://www.geocities.com:0080/Athens/Olympus/7583/adjposition.html>. ■

b Adverbs

Adverbs modify verbs, adjectives, or other adverbs, answering the questions *where? when?* and *how?* Many adverbs end in *-ly: The investment broker spoke **evasively.*** But some adverbs have both short and long forms: *quick/quickly.*

Use the *-ly* form in formal writing situations. For most academic and business audiences, you'll do better to use the long, *-ly* form. In more casual and colloquial writing, you can use the short forms.

STANDARD	We drive **slowly** in town.
COLLOQUIAL	Connie drives **slow.**
STANDARD	The employees asked to be treated **fairly.**
COLLOQUIAL	The employees asked to be treated **fair.**

Watch for double negatives. Using two *no* words—*no, not, nothing, nobody, never*—in the same sentence or independent clause is considered nonstandard. When you find you've used two of these words, usually you can just drop or change a single word.

That parrot ~~doesn't~~ never talk*s*.

John doesn't want ~~no~~ *any* help.

Similarly, don't mix the negative adverbs *hardly, scarcely,* or *barely* with another negative word or phrase.

could
The morning was so clear that the hikers ~~couldn't~~ hardly wait to get started.

However, to express an idea positively but with some reservation, you may use two negatives.

Well, I'm not **unhappy** about the new schedule.

c Comparatives and Superlatives

Adjectives and adverbs both have comparative forms and superlative forms. The comparative and superlative forms of most adjectives and adverbs can be expressed two ways.

ugly **(an adjective)**

COMPARATIVE	uglier	more ugly
SUPERLATIVE	ugliest	most ugly

slowly **(an adverb)**

COMPARATIVE	slower	more slowly
SUPERLATIVE	slowest	most slowly

Generally, add *-er* and *-est* endings to one-syllable adjectives and adverbs, but use the terms *more* and *most, less* and *least* before words of two or more syllables.

Camille talks **faster** than Susi.

Susi usually speaks **more deliberately.**

Use the comparative to compare two items.

smarter
Juan was the ~~smartest~~ of the two children.

more
Celeste, his twin, was the ~~most~~ imaginative.

Use the superlative to compare three or more items.

most
Given the choice of several toys, Celeste would choose the ~~more~~ challenging one.

Don't use double forms. Use only one form in a phrase.

Andre was ~~more~~ stricter as a parent than Lewona was.

Of the whole archery team, Diana was the ~~most~~ angriest about the stolen targets.

Grammar for ESL Writers

If you speak English as a second language, you may want to review Chapters 25–27 for strategies to find and correct common grammatical errors. In these chapters you will also find references to other sources of information—books, Web sites, and other sections of this handbook—that we recommend you consult for more extensive help with writing and grammar. Both ESL and native speakers of English may want to use Chapter 27, Proofreading in English, as a checklist for editing. ■

25 Nouns, Articles, and Quantifiers

*"Not everything that can be counted counts,
and not everything that counts can be
counted."*

—ALBERT EINSTEIN, physicist

Do you ever need help figuring out which article to use—*a, an,* or *the?* Do you know when no article should be used? Are you sometimes uncertain about whether to use *a few* or *a little* before some nouns? If so, this chapter will help you to distinguish between count and noncount nouns, and to select the articles and quantifiers that go with them.

EXPRESS!

When deciding whether to use a definite or indefinite article before a noun, ask yourself the following questions.

- Have I mentioned the noun before?
- Does the situation make the noun's specific identity clear?
- Have I used a phrase or clause after the noun that makes it specific?

If your response to any of these questions is "yes," and if you can also make the noun plural, you can probably use the definite article *the* before the noun.

a Count and Noncount Nouns

Nouns in English are either count nouns or noncount nouns. Count nouns are items that you can count or things that you can divide easily: *six books, sixty minutes.* Noncount nouns refer to things or ideas that cannot be counted or divided: *air, love, chemistry.*

Count nouns are singular (*finger*) or plural (*fingers*). Noncount nouns usually have only a single form: *gasoline.* You can often give a noncount noun a count meaning by adding a phrase such as *an instance of, a serving of,* or *a type of* before the noncount noun. In conversation, native speakers may omit the phrase, which can be confusing.

May we have three **waters,** please? (informal speech)

May we have three **glasses of water,** please? (full meaning)

Because you can't count noncount nouns, you can't use numbers or other expressions (*many, several*) that indicate numbers with noncount nouns.

EXAMPLES OF NONCOUNT NOUNS

Mass nouns: air, gasoline, plastic, rain, wood, wool
Food and drink: cheese, chocolate, coffee, fish, meat, milk, rice, tea, water
Abstract nouns: advice, beauty, employment, information, knowledge, satisfaction
Others: clothing, furniture, hair, homework, money, news, traffic, work

When you are unsure whether a noun is count or noncount, consult an ESL dictionary. See page 196 for a recommendation.

b Definite and Indefinite Articles

The or *a/an* **with a singular count noun.**   With a singular count noun, you need an article. As a rule, use the definite article when it is clear which specific thing you are referring to, and use the indefinite article when the reader or listener cannot be expected to know which particular item you mean.

1. **Use the indefinite article *a* or *an* when you introduce the noun for the first time, and once your reader understands the reference, use the definite article *the*.**

   There are several reasons why a person may end up homeless. Perhaps the person lost his or her job and could not pay for an apartment. Or perhaps the apartment was sold to a new owner who raised the rent. The new owner may not realize how expensive the rent is for that person.

2. **Use *the* when the noun is specified by a phrase or clause that follows it.**

   The book
   ~~Book~~ that I read is informative.

   The
   ~~A~~ book **on Robert Kennedy** is out.

3. **Use *the* with the superlative adjective.**

   the
   This is ^ best brand you can buy.

4. **Use *the* when the context makes it clear which specific thing is being referred to.**

   The earth
   ~~Earth~~ is round. (There is only one earth.)
   ^

   the
   Please take a̶ cake out of the oven. (Both speaker and listener
              ^
   know which cake.)

5. **When making generalizations, you can use either *a/an* or *the* with most singular count nouns.**

   A dog can be good company for **a** lonely **person.** (any dog;
   any lonely person)

   The computer has changed the banking industry dramati-
   cally. (the computer in general)

   The capitalist believes in free enterprise. (*The* is used to
   make general statements about specific species of animals or
   groups of people—e.g., capitalists.)

Use no article to make general statements with plural count nouns and noncount nouns.

Computers
~~The computers~~ have changed the banking industry dramati-
^
cally. (plural count noun)

Sugar
~~The sugar~~ is a major cause of tooth decay. (noncount noun)
^

c Quantifiers

The words that come before nouns and tell you *how much* or
how many are called *quantifiers*. Quantifiers are not always the
same for both count and noncount nouns.

- *Use with count and noncount nouns:* some, a lot of, plenty of,
  a lack of, most of the
- *Use with count nouns only:* several, many, a couple of, a few, few
- *Use with noncount nouns only:* a good deal of, a great deal of,
  (not) much, a little, little

Be careful to distinguish between *a few/a little* and *few/little*. With
the article, *a few* or *a little* means "not a lot, but enough."
Use *a few* with count nouns.

There are **a few books** in the library on capital punishment.

Use *a little* with noncount nouns.

> There is **a little information** in the library on capital punishment.

Without the article, *few* or *little* means "not enough."

> There are **few** female **leaders** in the world. (count noun; not enough female leaders)

> My mother has **little hope** that this will change. (noncount noun; not much hope)

<DESTINATIONS>

For quick reference charts and practice exercises for identifying count and noncount nouns, and the articles and quantifiers to use with them, visit the Purdue University *OWL* at <http://owl.english.purdue.edu/handouts/esl/eslcount.html>.

For lists of recommended Web resources in reading, writing, vocabulary, grammar, and other topics, organized by level, visit the *ESL Independent Study Lab* at Lewis & Clark University at <http://www.lclark.edu/~krauss/toppicks/toppicks.html>.

To explore a variety of topics to write about, as well as a well-rounded selection of other study areas, visit "Resources for English Language and Culture" at Ohio University's *Ohio ESL* at <http://www.ohiou.edu/esl/english/index.html>.

To find suggestions and strategies for investigating the English language on the Web, visit "Grammar Safari" at the Lingua-Center of the University of Illinois, Urbana-Champaign at <http://deil.lang.uiuc.edu/web.pages/grammarsafari.html#Common>. ■

26 Verbs and Verb Phrases

> *"For me, words are a form of action, capable of influencing change."*
> —INGRID BENGIS, writer

English verbs are complicated, and if you are a nonnative speaker, you probably still have questions about them, even after studying English for many years. This chapter addresses some of the trickier points of using verbs in English.

> ## EXPRESS!
>
> Learning to use English verbs correctly can be a daunting task. Equip yourself with a good grammar reference and an ESL dictionary so when questions arise, you can find the answers. Get in the habit, too, of jotting down verb phrases that you don't understand as you are reading and listening—and then search for their meaning in your reference books or ask your English-speaking friends for clarification.

Recommended Grammar and Usage References

Azar, Betty S. *Basic English Grammar (English as a Second Language)*. 3rd ed. New York: Longman, 2005.

Steer, Jocelyn, and Karen Carlisi. *The Advanced Grammar Book*. 2nd ed. New York: Newbury, 1997.

Recommended ESL Dictionary

Longman Dictionary of American English. 4th ed. New York: Pearson, 2008.

a Helping Verbs and Main Verbs

Helping verbs—*be, have, do,* and the modal auxiliary verbs (see page 245 in the glossary)—can be combined with main verbs to create tenses and to indicate different attitudes. Helping verbs (HV) always appear before main verbs (MV).

        HV HV   MV   HV   MV
The woman has been waiting for many hours. Do you want to wait?

When they are combined in a verb phrase, helping and main verbs always take this order:

> **Modal + form of *have* + form of *be* + main verb**

She could have   been   writing.

      Has she   started the letter yet?

***Have, be,* and *do*.** *Have, be,* and *do* change form to indicate tenses.

She **is** sleeping. She **has been** sleeping for three days. She **didn't** choose to.

1. *Have, has,* or *had* + **past participle.** Form the perfect tenses with *have* and the past participle (*-ed* form). See pages 170–173 for a list of the past participles of irregular verbs.

   Use the present perfect to indicate that an action may continue or still has the possibility of continuing in the future.

   I have ~~live~~ lived here for three months.

   My mother has never ~~uses~~ used a computer.

   Use the past perfect to indicate one action in the past that occurs before another action in the past.

   After they had ~~talk~~ talked about the plan for many weeks, they decided it wouldn't work.

2. **Form of** *be* + **present participle.** Form the progressive tenses with a form of *be*—*am, is, are, being, been, was, were*—and the present participle (*-ing* form). Use a progressive tense to indicate ongoing actions during a time period.

   Marge is ~~drive~~ driving the bus to San Francisco.

   While he was ~~study~~ studying the phone rang.

3. *Do, does,* or *did* + **base form.** *Do* is used in questions and negatives, or provides special emphasis in a sentence.

   Did they **carry** that heavy canoe for five miles?

   The weary traveler **didn't want** to cook. But she **did want** to eat.

Modals. Modal auxiliaries express an attitude about a situation. To be polite, for example, you can ask, "*Would* you open the door, please?" Choose the modal that best expresses your attitude.

   Permission (from informal to formal): *can, could, may, would you mind* (*if* + past tense)
   Ability: *can, be able to*
   Advice: *should, ought to, had better*
   Necessity: *have to, must*
   Lack of necessity: *not have to, not need to*
   Possibility (from more sure to less sure): *can, may, could, might*
   Conclusion: *must (have)*
   Expectation: *should, ought to*

Polite requests (from informal to formal): *can, will, could, would you mind* (+ *-ing*)

1. **Modal + base form of verb.**   Use the base form of a verb after a modal that expresses present or future time.

   Jacquie can ~~plays~~ the guitar very well.
   (play)

   In *have to, need to, be able to,* and *ought to,* retain the *to.*

   We **have to** write a ten-page paper.

2. **Modal +** *have* **+ past participle.**   Modals that give advice or express possibility, expectation, and conclusion have a perfect verb form. Use the perfect form to express past time.

   Where is Sue? She **should have been** here by now.

\<DESTINATION\>

For an excellent discussion and examples of English verb phrases from a linguist's point of view, visit Daniel Kies's *HyperTextBooks* at the College of DuPage at
\<http://papyr.com/hypertextbooks/engl_126/ph_verb.htm\>. ■

b | Gerunds and Infinitives

Both gerunds (*-ing* forms) and infinitives (*to* forms) can be used as the objects of verbs. However, certain verbs in English require that you use a gerund, not an infinitive, or an infinitive, not a gerund. Other verbs take both gerunds and infinitives as objects, but sometimes the form you choose changes the meaning of the sentence.

INFINITIVE   (*to* + base form of verb)

I want go with you.
(to)

GERUND   (base form of verb + *-ing*)

He enjoys ~~to jog~~ in the park.
(jogging)

Use an infinitive after these verbs.

afford, agree, appear, arrange, ask, beg, claim, consent, decide, deserve, expect, fail, hesitate, hope, intend, learn, manage, mean, need, offer, plan, pretend, promise, refuse, seem, threaten, wait, wish

Use a gerund after these verbs

admit, anticipate, appreciate, avoid, consider, delay, deny, discuss, dislike, enjoy, finish, can't help, keep, mention, miss, postpone, practice, quit, recall, recollect, recommend, resent, resist, risk, suggest, tolerate, understand

Use either a gerund or infinitive after these verbs. Your choice will not affect the meaning of the sentence.

begin, can't bear, can't stand, continue, hate, like, prefer, start

Use a gerund or infinitive, depending on your meaning

Try **to be** nice. (make an attempt to be nice)

Try **being** nice for a change. (do an experiment; you've never been nice before)

Did you remember **to wash** the car? (didn't forget to wash the car)

Do you remember **washing** the car last month? (do you recall washing the car)

Verbs like the following change their meaning when followed by an infinitive or a gerund.

forget (to be): not remember
(never) forget (being): always remember
regret (to be): feel sorry about
regret (being): feel sorry about a *past* action
remember (to be): not forget
remember (being): recall, bring to mind
stop (to be): stop in order to be
stop (being): interrupt an action
try (to be): make an attempt to be
try (being): do an experiment

Use a gerund after a preposition.

Carla has been worried about **passing** her statistics course.

Mrs. Short apologized for **interrupting** our conversation.

Follow transitive verbs with a noun or pronoun + infinitive.
A transitive verb is a verb that has a direct object. This means that
the verb has an effect on, or does something to, that object. The
object must be stated.

> *her*
> I told �‸ to write me a letter.

Transitive verbs include the following.

> advise, allow, cause, challenge, convince, encourage, forbid,
> force, hire, instruct, invite, order, persuade, remind, require,
> tell, urge, warn

Use the base form of the verb after *have, let,* **and** *make.*
Instead of being followed by an infinitive, these verbs are followed
by a noun or pronoun and the base form of the verb. Omit the *to*
before the verb.

> I had my mother ~~to~~ cut my hair.

c │ Two- and Three-Word Verbs

Some verbs in English consist of two or three words. These
verbs usually have a main verb and a preposition. These verbs are
idioms—you can't understand the meaning of the verb simply by
knowing the separate meaning of each of the two or three words.
For example, the verb *put off* ("to postpone") has a completely different meaning from *put up with* ("to tolerate"). *Look after* means
"to take care of," but *look into* means "to explore or investigate."

Two-word verbs that are transitive (take a direct object) are
either separable, meaning the object can be placed before or after
the preposition, or they are inseparable, meaning the verb and the
preposition cannot be separated.

> **SEPARABLE**   Lee **checked** the book out from the library.
>
> Lee **checked out** the book from the library.

But note that if the object is a pronoun, the pronoun *must*
come before the preposition.

> *it*
> Gary checked ˸ out ~~it~~ from the library.

> *up*
> **INSEPARABLE**   The frantic student stayed ˸ all night ~~up~~ to
> study.

> *look*
> Please ˸ after your brother ~~look.~~

Examples of Two- and Three-Word Verbs

Verb	Meaning
call off	cancel
come across*	encounter unintentionally
cut down on*	reduce the amount of
do over	repeat
figure out	solve a problem
get along with*	have harmonious relations
keep up with*	maintain the same level
make up	invent
pick out	make a selection
run into*	meet by chance
show up*	appear, arrive
stand up for*	defend, support
take after*	resemble, look alike

Inseparable

There are many other two- and three-word verbs in English in addition to these.

27 Proofreading in English

"I've never seen a monument erected for a pessimist."
—Paul Harvey, broadcast journalist

Always proofread your papers carefully before you hand in the final copy. Here is a list of common proofreading problems and their solutions; add your own typical problems, and then check for them each time you proofread a paper.

1. **Does every clause have a subject? (Exception: commands such as "Sit down!")**

   It is challenging to write in English.

2. **Are any sentence elements repeated unnecessarily?**

   ADJECTIVE CLAUSES   The store that I told you about ~~it~~
   closed down.

SUBJECTS — My brother ~~he~~ is the director of the hospital.

MULTIPLE CONNECTORS — Although the employee was diligent, ~~but~~ she was fired.

3. **Are all necessary helping verbs and main verbs included?**

The teacher ^*was* extremely helpful.

The plane ^*is* leaving right now.

4. **Do all verbs used with third-person singular nouns and pronouns end in *-s*?**

The library close ^*s* at 5:00 today.

5. **Do all past participles end in *-ed*?** (See pages 170–173 for a list of verbs with irregular past participles.)

PASSIVE VOICE — The documents were alter ^*ed* by the thief.

PAST PERFECT TENSE — Juan had finish ^*ed* the race before Chuck came.

PARTICIPLE ADJECTIVES — She was frighten ^*ed* by the dark.

6. **Are *-ing* endings on adjectives used for active meanings, and *-ed* endings for passive meanings?** (See page 175 for an explanation of passive voice.)

Her work is satisfying. Joan does satisfying work. (active)

She is satisfied by her work. She is a satisfied employee. (passive)

Check These Pairs
amusing/amused by
annoying/annoyed by
boring/bored by
confusing/confused by
embarrassing/embarrassed by
exciting/excited by (or about)
frightening/frightened by
interesting/interested in
irritating/irritated by
satisfying/satisfied with

7. **Are adverbs placed correctly?**

Adverbs can't be placed between a verb and its object.

She answered ~~slowly~~ the question.
slowly ^

Adverbs of frequency can't be placed before the verb *be*.

Louise ~~regularly~~ is late for class.
regularly ^

Adverbs of frequency can't be placed after other verbs.

Harold arrives ~~often~~ late to class.
often ^

ESL Index

You probably have other questions about English grammar or punctuation that we haven't covered in this part of *SF Express*— questions that native speakers also ask. Find your topic in this index, or check the index in the back of the book.

Punctuation and Mechanics

206 28a
Commas

28 Commas

"A kiss can be a comma, a question mark, or an exclamation point."

—MISTINGUETT, dancer

EXPRESS!

Every comma in a sentence should be placed for a reason: to mark a pause, to set off a unit, to keep words from running together. As signals, commas aren't as strong as semicolons, which typically appear at major intersections between clauses. And they are certainly not as forceful as periods, which mark the ends of sentences. Instead, commas make a reader slow down and pay attention to the words and ideas they set off. For this reason, it's just as important to omit commas where they aren't needed as it is to include them where they are.

a Before a Coordinating Conjunction in a Compound Sentence

Coordinating conjunctions—*and, or, nor, for, but, yet,* and *so*—link independent clauses. Clauses are described as *independent* when they can stand on their own as sentences. Joining two independent clauses with a comma and a coordinating conjunction produces a compound sentence.

West Texas can seem empty‸yet the vastness of its high plains is part of its appeal.

Do not put the comma after the conjunction, a common error.

My friends shared my opinion‸but̷they were afraid to say so.

Do not use a comma alone to link independent clauses. Linking independent clauses with a comma alone produces the error called a *comma splice*. Add a conjunction to indicate the relationship between the clauses.

The plane to Atlanta was late,‸^so^we missed our connecting flight to Indianapolis.

b | After an Introductory Word Group

Phrases.   Commas are generally used after introductory phrases of more than three or four words.

> To appreciate the pleasures of driving in snow‸you have to live in Michigan or Wisconsin.

> Over the loud objections of all the Jeep's occupants‸I turned off the main road.

When an introductory phrase is short and the sentence is clear without the punctuation, you can omit the comma, although you won't be wrong to include it.

> For now I'll abstain from voting.

Use a comma to help avoid confusion or misreading—for example, after an introductory prepositional phrase or verbal.

> Stranded‸the hikers headed due south.
> In Louisiana‸state laws are still influenced by the Napoleonic Code.

Clauses.   Always use a comma after an introductory subordinate clause. Subordinate clauses are signaled by words such as *although, if, when, because, as, after, before, since, unless,* and *while.*

> Although the vote was close‸we passed the motion.

c | With Nonrestrictive Modifiers

Use commas to mark nonrestrictive (nonessential) modifiers. A nonrestrictive, or nonessential, modifier is one that adds information to a sentence but can be removed without radically altering its basic meaning. Observe what happens when nonessential modifiers are removed from some sentences; some information is lost, but good sense is maintained.

Adjective phrases

WITH COMMAS— **NONRESTRICTIVE**	The police officers, who looked sharp in their dress uniforms, marched in front of the mayor's car.
LOGICAL WITHOUT **MODIFIER**	The police officers marched in front of the mayor's car.

Do not use commas around restrictive, or essential, modifiers. Restrictive modifiers cannot be removed from a sentence without affecting its meaning. When an essential modifier is removed from a sentence, the sense of the sentence is lost.

NO COMMAS— RESTRICTIVE	Diamonds that are synthetically produced are more perfect than natural diamonds.
NOT LOGICAL	Diamonds are more perfect than natural diamonds.

A good general rule: Any clause introduced by *that* will be restrictive and should not be surrounded by commas.

The committee‿that I chair‿meets every Monday.

Appositives.   An appositive—a noun or noun equivalent that follows a noun and gives additional information about it—can be restrictive or nonrestrictive. Use commas to enclose only nonrestrictive (nonessential) appositives.

Colleen O'Brien ‿our neighborhood-watch coordinator ‿was arrested last week for shoplifting.

Tom Robbins's novel‿*Half Asleep in Frog Pajamas*‿demonstrates Robbins's talent for using words creatively to reveal their underlying origins and metaphors.

d   To Set Off Contrasts and Transitional Expressions

Use commas to mark contrasting elements and transitional expressions (including conjunctive adverbs such as *however, moreover, therefore,* and *nevertheless*).

Owning a car in most cities is a necessity ‿not a luxury.

Althea studied hard; therefore ‿she passed the examination easily.

When a contrasting clause comes after a main clause, use a comma to set it off. Also set off elements that follow a main clause when the additional thought is incidental or additional. Such clauses may be signaled by words such as *although, though, if, when, because, as, after, before, since, unless, while,* and *that is.*

We will attend the judge's lecture ‿which is scheduled to last an hour.

When the additional clause is closely related to the main idea of the sentence, commas are not used. This is often a judgment call; writers won't agree in every case.

The flag was lowered while the military band played taps.

The police officers found the window broken when they arrived.

e To Set Off Parenthetical Elements, Interjections, Direct Address, and Tag Questions

When these interruptions come in the middle of a sentence, be sure to set them off with a pair of commas.

The senators it seems are eager for a filibuster.

It is interesting Ms. Howard that your story differs so much from Ms. Liu's.

So you believe the world is flat do you?

f To Set Off Absolute Phrases

Absolutes are phrases made up of nouns and participles.

His head shaved Martin was in the Marines now.

The pioneers pressed forward across the desert their water almost gone.

g With Items in a Series

Use commas to link more than two items in a series. Commas keep the items in a series from colliding.

The mapmaker had omitted the capital cities of Idaho New York and Delaware!

Use commas to link coordinate adjectives in a series. Coordinate adjectives modify the noun they precede, not each other. If adjectives can be linked with the word *and,* they are coordinate. Coordinates can also be switched around without major changes in meaning.

David is a sarcastic, vindictive, and slightly frazzled secretary.

David is a vindictive, slightly frazzled, and sarcastic secretary.

In contrast, do not use commas between noncoordinate adjectives in a series. Noncoordinate adjectives work together to modify a term. They cannot be switched around or have *and* inserted between them.

> He drives a shiny blue Mustang.

h With Quotations

> "Experience," said Oscar Wilde "is the name everyone gives to their mistakes."

> Said P. G. Wodehouse "I always advise people never to give advice."

i In Dates, Addresses, and Numbers

Dates. In American usage, commas separate the day from the year. A year is enclosed by commas if it appears in the middle of a sentence.

> Germany expanded World War II on June 22, 1941 when its armies invaded Russia.

Commas aren't required when only the month and year are given.

> World War II began in September 1939.

Addresses. Commas ordinarily separate street addresses, cities, states, and countries. When these items occur in the middle of a sentence, they are enclosed by commas.

> Though born in London, England Denise Levertov is considered an American writer.

Commas aren't used between states and zip codes.

> Austin, Texas 78712

Numbers. Commas separate units of three but are optional in four-digit numbers.

> 4,110 or 4110

> 1,235,470

Do not use commas in decimals, social security numbers, street addresses, telephone numbers, or zip codes.

j | Unnecessary Commas

No comma separates a subject from a verb. This common error usually occurs when the full subject is more complex than usual.

> What happened to the team since last season‸isn't clear.

What happened to the team is the subject of the sentence, so it shouldn't be separated from the verb *is* with a comma.

No comma separates compound subjects, predicates, or objects.

> The Mississippi‸and the Missouri are two of the United States' great rivers.

> We toured the museum‸and then explored the monument.

> Alexander broke his promise to his agent‸and his contract with his publisher.

No comma introduces a series. If any punctuation mark is needed, it will usually be a colon, not a comma.

> States with impressive national parks include‸California, Utah, Arizona, and New Mexico.

No commas around essential modifiers. When a modifying phrase is essential, it should not be set off with commas (see 28c).

> What Asha observed‸as a civic volunteer‸changed her opinion of journalists.

29 Semicolons and Colons

"An idea is a feat of association."
—ROBERT FROST, poet

EXPRESS!

Using semicolons is more a matter of style than grammatical correctness. Strictly speaking, a period can almost always replace a

(continued)

semicolon in joining two independent clauses. However, a period declares a full stop between two sentences, whereas a semicolon suggests a slowing down, a pause. A semicolon signals to readers that the two sentences on either side of the semicolon are closely related in thought.

a   Semicolons

Use semicolons when you need punctuation stronger than a comma but weaker than a period.

To link related independent clauses.   Often the clause after a semicolon will clarify, add information to, or contrast with the clause before the semicolon.

Give Matthew the book_; it belongs to him.

To set off conjunctive adverbs and transitions.   Independent clauses can be joined by conjunctive adverbs such as *however, therefore, nevertheless, moreover,* and *consequently,* and transitional expressions such as *indeed, in fact, at any rate, for example, as a result,* and *on the other hand.* When they are, use a semicolon before the expression.

Good films often spawn sequels_; however, the sequels rarely match the originals in quality.

The film's prerelease publicity had been enormous. _{; as} A result, opening-day crowds broke all records.

Caution: Using a comma instead of a semicolon in these situations produces a comma splice—a serious punctuation error.

To separate items in a list that contains commas or other punctuation.

Bob Hope's films include *Road to Morocco,* which also features Bing Crosby and Dorothy Lamour_; *The Paleface,* a comic western with Jane Russell as Calamity Jane_; and *The Seven Little Foys,* a biography about vaudeville performer Eddie Foy, Sr.

Unnecessary semicolons.

NO SEMICOLON BETWEEN A DEPENDENT AND INDEPENDENT CLAUSE

Although director Alfred Hitchcock once said that actors should be treated like cattle; he won fine performances from many of them.

NO SEMICOLON BETWEEN AN INDEPENDENT CLAUSE AND A PREPOSITIONAL PHRASE

In the tradition of the finest Hollywood directors; many young filmmakers regularly exceed their budgets.

NO SEMICOLON TO INTRODUCE A LIST

Paul Robeson performed in several distinguished films; *Showboat, Song of Freedom,* and *King Solomon's Mines.*

b Colons

Use colons to point to ideas, lists, quotations, or clauses you wish to emphasize. A colon always follows an independent clause.

To direct readers to examples, explanations, or significant words or phrases.

Orson Welles's greatest problem may also have been his greatest achievement; the brilliance of his first film, *Citizen Kane.*

Making a film is like writing a paper, It absorbs all the time you can give it.

To direct readers to lists after independent clauses.

Besides *Citizen Kane,* Welles directed, produced, or acted in many movies; *The Magnificent Ambersons, Journey into Fear,* and *Macbeth,* to name a few.

Don't use colons after expressions such as *for example, such as, including,* or *that is.* The colon is intended to replace these expressions.

Shoestring budgets have produced many successful films such as; *My Big Fat Greek Wedding, The Blair Witch Project,* and *Good Will Hunting.*

However, colons are used after phrases that more specifically an-
nounce a list, such as *including these, as follows,* and *such as the
following.*

Don't use colons after linking verbs or between a preposition
and its object.

Among the many successful films produced on shoestring
budgets are ʲMy Big Fat Greek Wedding, The Blair Witch Project, and Good Will Hunting.

Katharine Hepburn starred inʲ Little Women, The Philadel-
phia Story, and The African Queen.

To direct readers to pay special attention to quotations or dialogue.

We recalled Dirty Harry's memorable challenge; "Make my
day!"

However, use commas with most dialogue labels or tags.

As Dirty Harry said: "Make my day!"

To separate titles from subtitles, numbers in time expressions, and chapter and verse in biblical passages.
Colons also follow the salutation in business letters.

"Darkest Night: Hollywood and *Film Noir*"

12:35 p.m.

Matthew 3:1 (but in MLA style, Matthew 3.1)

Dear Mr. Ebert:

e-TIPS

"Smileys," or "emoticons," are characters created from various typographical elements. These may appear in email or other electronic
environments to express feelings or opinions ranging from delight to
surprise to disapproval. Emoticons should typically be reserved for
informal communications.

smiley face	: -)
frowney face	: - (
wink	; -)
bored	: -|
yawn	: - o
hug	[]

30   Quotation Marks

"Next to the originator of a good sentence is the first quoter of it."

—RALPH WALDO EMERSON,
philosopher and essayist

Quotation marks, which always occur in pairs, highlight what appears between them—namely titles, dialogue, and specific words.

EXPRESS!

Titles to be enclosed in quotation marks include the following. For a list of titles that appear in *italic* (or underlined), see page 221.

chapters of books	"Lessons from the Pros"
magazine articles	"Is the Stock Market Too High?"
journal articles	"Vai Script and Literacy"
newspaper articles	"Inflation Heats Up"
newspaper sections	"Living in Style"
TV episodes	"Homer's Night Out"
radio episodes	"McGee Goes Crackers"
short stories	"Araby"
short poems	"The Red Wheelbarrow"
songs	"The Star-Spangled Banner"

a   To Set Off Direct Quotations

Around short selections borrowed word for word from sources. In MLA documentation (Chapter 11), quotation marks go before the parenthetical citation. (See pages 70 and 73, especially 11c, on indicating omissions to quoted material and on introducing and framing quotations.)

According to Kathleen Hall Jamieson, a memorable phrase can sum up a speech and become "the hook on which we hang it in memory" (90).

Note: Borrowed material that is longer than four lines (in MLA style) or more than forty words (in APA style) is not enclosed by quotation marks. Instead, these longer passages are handled as block quotations. (See page 73 for MLA; page 113 for APA.)

e-TIPS

Your email program probably does not use quotation marks to distinguish between your current message and a message you may be responding to. Instead, it usually marks the copied material with a vertical line or other typographical device, typically in the left margin.

To mark dialogue.   When writing a passage with several speakers, start a new paragraph each time the speaker changes.

> "Kitty has no discretion in her coughs," said her father; "she times them ill."
>
> "I do not cough for my own amusement," replied Kitty fretfully.   —Jane Austen, *Pride and Prejudice*

With quotations introduced, interrupted, or followed by *said, remarked, observed,* or a similar expression.

> Benjamin Disraeli observed, "It is much easier to be critical than to be correct."
>
> "If the world were a logical place," Rita Mae Brown notes, "men would ride sidesaddle."

In quotations within quotations.   Use double quotation marks (" ") around most quoted material; use single quotation marks (' ') to mark quotations within quotations.

> Jane said, "I love folk songs from the 1960s."
>
> Jane said, "My favorite is 'If I Had a Hammer.'"

b To Cite the Titles of Short Works

These include titles of songs, essays, magazine and newspaper articles, TV episodes, unpublished speeches, chapters of books, and short poems (see Express! page 215). Titles of longer works appear in *italic* (see Express! page 221).

> "Love Is Just a Four-Letter Word" [song]

c | With Other Punctuation Marks

After commas and periods.   Place commas and periods inside closing quotation marks, except when you are using MLA documentation (see page 73).

> "There is no such thing as a moral book or an immoral book," says Oscar Wilde. "Books are well-written or badly written. That is all."

> MLA STYLE
>
> Mike Rose argues that we hurt education if we think of it "in limited or limiting ways" (3).

Before colons and semicolons.   Place colons and semicolons outside closing quotation marks.

> Riley claimed to be "a human calculator": He did quadratic equations in his head.

> The young Cassius Clay bragged about being "the greatest"; his opponents in the ring soon learned he wasn't boasting.

With question marks, exclamation points, and dashes. These punctuation marks can fall either inside or outside the closing quotation marks. They fall inside when they apply only to the quotation.

> When Mrs. Rattle saw her hotel room, she muttered, "Good grief!"

> She turned to her husband and said, "Do you really expect me to stay here?"

They fall outside the closing quotation mark when they apply to the complete sentence.

> Who was it who said, "Truth is always the strongest argument"?

Other quotations.   No extra punctuation is required when a quotation runs smoothly into a sentence you have written.

> Abraham Lincoln observed that "in giving freedom to the slave we assure freedom to the free."

d | To Draw Attention to Specific Words or Expressions

People clearly mean different things when they write about "democracy."

Use quotation marks to show when you are using words or expressions ironically, sarcastically, or derisively. But don't overdo the use of quotation marks for adding emphasis; doing so makes your text harder to read.

The clerk at the desk directed the tourists to their "suites"— bare rooms crowded with cots. A bathroom down the hall would serve as the "spa."

31 Apostrophes

"If the English language made any sense, a catastrophe would be an apostrophe with fur."
—DOUG LARSON

EXPRESS!

Probably the most common apostrophe errors occur with *its/it's* and *whose/who's*. Most writers form the contractions—*it's* and *who's*— correctly. The mistakes come with the possessive forms—*its* and *whose*—because these forms deviate from the general rule of adding an apostrophe and *-s* to a singular noun.

ITS = POSSESSIVE

The dog injured its leg.

The cat licked its whiskers.

IT'S = CONTRACTION

It's time to go. (It is time to go.)

WHOSE = POSSESSIVE

Whose watch is this?

Whose house is this?

WHO'S = CONTRACTION

Who's going to the movie? (Who is going to the movie?)

a | To Form Possessive Nouns

Add an apostrophe + -s to most singular nouns and to plural nouns that do not end in -s.

> a dog's life
>
> geese's behavior
>
> the NCAA's ruling
>
> children's imaginations

Form the possessive of singular nouns ending in -s or -z with either an apostrophe + -s or just the apostrophe. Use one form or the other consistently.

> the countess's jewels *or* the countess' jewels
>
> Katz's menu or Katz' menu

Add an apostrophe (but not an -s) to plural nouns that end in -s.

> the hostesses' job
>
> the senators' parking spaces

Do not use apostrophes to make personal pronouns possessive. Personal pronouns include *my, your, her, his, our, their,* and *its.* Don't confuse the possessive pronouns *its* and *whose* with the contractions *it's* and *who's.*

> **It's** an idea that has **its** opponents up in arms.
>
> **Who's** to say **whose** opinion is right?

Use apostrophes to show possession in compound or hyphenated words. Add the apostrophe to the last word in the compound item.

> the president-elect's decision
>
> both fathers-in-law's Cadillacs

b | In Contractions and Omissions

Use apostrophes in contractions to show where letters have been omitted. Such apostrophes are not optional.

> can't—cannot
>
> it's—it is or it has

you're—you are

who's—who is or who has

c In Some Plurals

The apostrophe is optional to form the plurals of numbers, symbols, individual letters, abbreviations, dates, and words used as words. Use an apostrophe when needed for the sake of clarity, but avoid an apostrophe when the -*'s* might be mistaken for a possessive.

2's and 3's or 2s and 3s	the 1940's or the 1940s
A's and B's or As and Bs	and's or *ands*
B.A.'s or B.A.s	the three CEO's or the three CEOs
two CD's or two CDs	The ACT's or the ACTs

Do not use apostrophes to form the plurals of nouns.

The company can put up sign~~'~~s in the neighborhood.

Do not use apostrophes to form the plurals of family names.   Form such plurals by adding an -*s* or -*es*. Form possessives by adding an apostrophe.

Singular	**Plural**	**Possessive**
Richard Clarke	the Clarkes	the Clarkes' dog
Jean James	the Jameses	the Jameses' house

d To Show Joint Ownership

When two nouns share ownership, only the second noun needs an apostrophe.

Peg and John's research grant

Vorhees and Goetz' project

When ownership is separate, each noun shows possession. In such cases, the objects possessed are usually plural.

Peg's and John's educations

Vorhees' and Goetz' offices

32 Other Punctuation Marks

"I personally think we developed language because of our deep need to complain."
—LILY TOMLIN, comic, actress

EXPRESS!

Titles that appear in *italic* (or underlined) include the following. For a list of titles that are enclosed in quotation marks, see page 215.

books	*All the Pretty Horses*
magazines	*Slate*
journals	*Written Communication*
newspapers	*New York Times*
films	*Casablanca*
TV shows	*The Tonight Show*
radio shows	*All Things Considered*
plays	*Measure for Measure*
long poems	*Paradise Lost*
long musical pieces	*The Mikado*
albums	Beck's *Odelay*
paintings	Schnabel's *Adieu*
sculptures	Christo's *Running Fence*
dances	Antonio's *Goya*
ships	U.S.S. *Saratoga*
trains	the *Orient Express*
aircraft	*Enola Gay*
spacecraft	*Apollo 11*
software programs	*Microsoft Word*

a Periods

Use periods to mark the end of sentences and abbreviations.

To end statements and most commands.

Hannibal, general of Carthage, has been hailed as a genius of military strategy.

Just look at the dog.

To end indirect questions. Indirect questions are statements that seem to have questions within them. They usually contain the words *whether* or *if,* or an interrogative pronoun such as *which* or *who.*

> Varro wondered whether Hannibal's strategy would succeed.
>
> Martha wants to know which window keeps getting stuck.

To punctuate most abbreviations. Most abbreviations for one- or two-word expressions require periods, but post office state abbreviations do not.

anon.	Ms.	Dr.	Ph.D.
U.S.	WI	CA	TX

Longer abbreviations written in capital letters often don't require periods.

FBI	CIA	UNICEF	NAFTA
NOW	MADD	NATO	

To indicate decimals.

> 0.01 $189.99   75.47

e-TIPS

Addresses for World Wide Web sites include a number of conventional marks, such as periods (called "dots"), colons, and slashes. Email addresses typically include the symbol for *at*: @.

WORLD WIDE WEB ADDRESS

http://www.uwyo.edu/

EMAIL ADDRESS

feedback@sss.whitehouse.gov

In MLA documentation, electronic addresses are enclosed in angle brackets to prevent surrounding punctuation from being mistakenly attached to the item.

<http://www.utexas.edu/>

b   Question Marks

Use question marks to terminate questions or to suggest doubt.

After direct questions.

> Who fought in the Battle of Cannae?

To indicate uncertainty about dates, numbers, or statements.

> Hannibal (247?–183 B.C.) was a military tactician.

> She survived that terrible crash?

To end sentences that begin as statements but end with direct questions.

> The strategy looked fine, but would it work on the battlefield?

Don't confuse this construction with an indirect question, discussed in 32a.

With quotation marks.   Place question marks outside quotation marks except when they are part of the quoted material itself.

> Was it Terence who wrote "Fortune helps the brave"?

> "Have you read any Cicero?" the teacher asked.

c Exclamation Points

Although rare in academic and business writing, exclamation points give emphasis to statements. Use only one exclamation point in a sentence.

> Don't overdo it!!!!

To express strong feelings or commands.

> Oh, no! We're lost again.   Come here now!

Don't use commas after exclamations that fall in the middle of sentences.

> "Please check your records again!" the caller demanded.

d Dashes

Use dashes to separate and call attention to ideas in sentences.

To insert a comment or call attention to information in a sentence.   Dashes in the middle of a sentence are always paired.

> Marie's writing style—complex, subtle, yet also incisive—earned the admiration of her colleagues.

To emphasize illustrations, examples, or summaries, or to call attention to a shift or contrast in content or tone.

> Beethoven's Ninth Symphony was a great accomplishment for an artist in bad health—and completely deaf.

> I'm heartened that Beck, Lou, and others are apparently able to look at the positive side of the experience—and envious.
> —Jon Krakauer, *Into Thin Air*

Don't use a hyphen when a dash is required. Use hyphens to connect items; use dashes to separate items. On most computer keyboards, you can type a dash with a key combination. Or, you can type a dash using two unspaced hyphens [--]. Do not leave spaces before or after a dash.

> Beethoven's music—unlike that of Mozart—uses emphatic rhythms.

Don't use too many dashes in a sentence or passage. Certainly use no more than one pair of dashes per sentence.

> Mozart—recognized as a genius while still a child—produced more than 600 compositions during his life—including symphonies, operas, and concertos.

e Hyphens

Use hyphens either to put words together or to divide them between syllables.

To link some compound nouns and verbs. The conventions for hyphenating words are complicated and inconsistent. The following are some expressions that take hyphens and some that don't. When in doubt, check a dictionary or style manual.

best-seller	mother-in-law	right-hander	cab owner
best man	life span	cabdriver	

To indicate double titles, elements, functions, or attributes.

city-state	space-time	AFL-CIO

To link unit modifiers before a noun. A *unit modifier* is a two-word modifier in which the first word modifies the second. The resulting unit modifies a following noun.

an English-speaking city   a hard-hitting exposé

When a comma between the modifying words produces nonsense, you probably have a unit modifier that requires a hyphen.

an English, speaking city (?)

But don't use hyphens to link compound modifiers following a noun.

The candidate was hardly awe̶-inspiring.

Don't use hyphens with *very* or with adverbs that end in *-ly.*

a very̶-hot day   a sharply̶-honed knife

In numbers from twenty-one to ninety-nine, and in fractions.

two hundred forty-six   one forty-seventh of a mile

To link prefixes to proper nouns and their corresponding adjectives.

pre-Columbian   anti-American

mid-Victorian   neo-Darwinism

In all words beginning with the prefixes *all-, self-,* and *ex-* or ending with the suffix *-elect.*

all-encompassing   ex-hockey player

self-contained   mayor-elect

Hyphenate most words beginning with *well-, ill-,* and *heavy-.*

well-dressed   ill-suited   heavy-handed

Most common nouns beginning with *un-, non-, anti-, pro-, co-,* and *pre-* are not hyphenated.

uncertainty   antislavery

coordination   prodemocracy

e-TIPS

To avoid hyphenating words or numbers at the ends of lines, turn on the word wrap function of your word processor. The word wrap will automatically eliminate end-of-line divisions. When you must divide a word, break it only at a syllable and then check a dictionary for the syllable break.

f | Ellipses

Use an ellipsis (. . .) to mark a gap in a sentence or passage. Type an ellipsis using three periods or dots with spaces between them.

Where material has been omitted from direct quotations. This material may be a word, a phrase, a sentence, or more. See 11c for MLA guidelines for using ellipses in quotations.

To be honest . . . is to be one man picked out of ten thousand.
—*Hamlet* 2.2

To indicate pauses or to suggest that an action is incomplete or continuing.

The rocket rumbled on its launch pad as the countdown proceeded: "Four, three, two, . . ."

To indicate that a speaker is hesitating or that a speech has trailed off.

"If you insist . . . ," the clerk muttered.

Spacing and punctuation. Use correct spacing and punctuation before and after ellipsis marks. When an ellipsis mark appears in the middle of a sentence, leave a space before the first period and after the last period.

chords of memory . . . will yet swell

If a punctuation mark occurs immediately before the ellipsis, include the mark when it makes your sentence easier to read. Then, add a space and the ellipsis.

We are not enemies, . . . must not be enemies.

When an ellipsis occurs at the end of a complete sentence or when you delete a full sentence or more, place a period at the end of the sentence, followed by a space and then the ellipsis.

We must not be enemies. . . . The mystic chords

Use an ellipsis at the beginning of a quotation only when an incomplete sentence might be mistaken for a full one because the quoted passage opens with a capital letter.

As Falstaff puts it, ". . . God help the wicked!"

g Parentheses

Enclose extra information, a comment, or an aside in parentheses. Parentheses are less emphatic than dashes and more common than brackets.

To separate material—a word, phrase, list, or complete sentence—from the main body of a sentence or paragraph.

The flight to Colorado was quick (ninety minutes) and uneventful.

To highlight numbers or letters used to list items within the text.

The labor negotiators realized they could (1) concede on all issues immediately, (2) stonewall until the public demanded a settlement, or (3) hammer out a compromise.

With end punctuation. Place parentheses properly either inside or outside end punctuation. When a complete sentence standing alone is surrounded by parentheses, its end punctuation belongs *inside* the end parenthesis.

The neighborhood was run-down and littered. (Some houses hadn't been painted in decades.)

When a sentence concludes with parentheses, the end punctuation for the complete sentence falls *outside* the final parentheses mark.

On the corner was a small church (actually, a converted store).

To provide source information in MLA and APA documentation. For guidelines and examples, see 11a (MLA) and 12a (APA).

To set off acronyms. For the first mention of an agency or organization, use the full name and indicate the appropriate acronym in parentheses. Then you can use the acronym in the rest of your paper.

As law has become a popular professional choice, college graduates flock in increasing numbers to testing sites for the Law School Admissions Test (LSAT). The LSAT measures

logical and analytical reasoning, reading comprehension,
and writing.

—Myra and David Sadker, *Failing at Fairness:*
How Our Schools Cheat Girls

h Brackets

Use brackets for special situations.

To insert comments or explanations into direct quotations.
You cannot change the words in a direct quotation, but you can
add information in brackets.

"He [George Lucas] reminded me a little of Walt Disney's
version of a mad scientist."   —Steven Spielberg

Any change to an original text, even if only from an uppercase
to a lowercase letter or vice versa, should be signaled with brackets.

In *The Dinosaur Heresies,* Bakker rejects "[o]rthodox theory."
Dinosaurs, he argues, are not just big reptiles with a "metab-
olism [that is] pitifully low compared to mammals'."

To avoid one set of parentheses falling within another.
Turn the inner pair into brackets.

The paper included a full text of the resolution (expressing
the sense of the House of Representatives on the calculation
of the Consumer Price Index [H.RES.99]).

**To acknowledge or highlight errors that originate in quoted
material.**   Enclose the word *sic* in brackets immediately after the
error.

The sign said, "We except [*sic*] no checks."

i Italics (Underlining)

Use italics or underlining to draw attention to a title, a word,
or a phrase.

To set off some titles.   In general, italicize titles of works that are
published as independent units, such as books, magazines, journals,
newspapers, films, TV shows, plays, long poems, paintings,
sculptures, and software programs (see Express! page 221). Titles of
shorter works appear in quotation marks (see Express! page 215).
Also italicize the names of ships, trains, aircraft, and spacecraft.

Do not use italics or quotation marks with titles of major religious texts, books of the bible, or classic legal documents.

the Bible | Genesis
the Qur'an | the Declaration of Independence

e-TIPS

When email will not permit underlining or italics, writers use an *underscore* (shift + hyphen) before and after a book title or other expression that would normally be italicized. Other punctuation follows the underscore.

Everyone in the newsgroup might enjoy reading a review of _The DaVinci Code_ that appeared in this week's _New York Times_.

To set off foreign words and phrases.
Latin names for biological categories such as genus and species are also italicized.

Environmental problems haunt the *maquiladora* corridor along the U.S.–Mexican border.

Mary and Louis Leakey pioneered the search for the ancestors of *Homo sapiens.*

To set off words, letters, numbers, and phrases referred to as themselves, not as what they stand for.
You can use quotation marks instead, if you prefer.

Does that word begin with an *f* or a *ph*?

The word *weird* is often misspelled.

To emphasize a letter, word, or phrase.

"That may be how *you* play volleyball," she replied.

j Slashes

Slashes are used for a few specific functions.

To divide lines of poetry quoted within sentences.
Leave a space on either side of the slash.

Only then does Lear understand that he has been a failure as a king: "O, I have taken / Too little care of this!"

If you quote more than three lines of verse, set the passage as a block quotation and break the lines as they appear in the poem itself. Do not use slashes.

To separate expressions that indicate a choice.   Leave no space before or after the slash.

yes/no   pass/fail

33 Capital Letters, Abbreviations, and Numbers

"In order to make an apple pie from scratch, you must first create the universe."
—CARL SAGAN, astronomer

EXPRESS!

To capitalize a title, follow these three steps.
- Capitalize the first word.
- Capitalize the last word.
- Capitalize all other words *except*

    Articles (*a, an, the*)
    The *to* in infinitives (*to* grow)
    Prepositions (*in, at, on,* and so forth)
    Coordinating conjunctions (*and, but, or, for, yet, so*)

---

a Capital Letters

Capitalize the first word of a sentence.

It was a dark and stormy night.

Capitalize the first word of a direct quotation when it is a full sentence.   Use lowercase for quotations that continue after an interruption.

Ira asked, "Where's the Air and Space museum?"

"It's on the Mall," the guide replied, "not far from the Hirschhorn Gallery."

Don't capitalize the first word after a colon unless you want to emphasize it or unless it is part of a title.

NO CAPITAL	They ignored one detail while parking the car: a no-parking sign.
ADDED EMPHASIS	The words haunted her: Your license has expired!
PART OF TITLE	*Marilyn: The Untold Story*

Capitalize the major words in the titles of books, papers, articles, poems, and so on.

All the Trouble in the World
"Stopping by Woods on a Snowy Evening"

Capitalize the first word in lines of quoted poetry unless the poet has used lowercase letters.

Sumer is ycomen in,

Loude sing cuckoo!

—"The Cuckoo Song"

anyone lived in a pretty how town,

(with up so floating many bells down)

—E. E. Cummings, "anyone lived in a pretty how town"

Capitalize the names and titles of people.   People's names are *proper nouns,* which refer to specific people, places, or things, while nouns that refer to people, places, and things in general are called *common nouns.*

Proper Nouns	Common Nouns
Emily Dickinson	poet
John	brother
Ted Kennedy	senator

Also capitalize titles associated with people.

Justice Ruth Ginsberg   Rosa Eberly, Ph.D.
R. Donald King, Dean of Liberal Arts

It is generally acceptable to capitalize a title that is being used in place of a name.

> the President or the president
> the Secretary of State or the secretary of state

Capitalize titles of family members if the titles are standing in place of names. Compare the two examples.

> Every night, Mother expected us to read ten pages from Jane Austen or Charles Dickens before watching television.

> My mother insisted that we read good literature.

Capitalize *God* when you are referring specifically to the god of the Judeo-Christian tradition, but not when you are referring to *gods* in general.

> In the Old Testament, God punished those who chose to worship the pagan gods.

Capitalize the names of national, political, or ethnic groups.

> Kenyans
> Australians
> African Americans

Capitalize the names of institutions and specific objects.

businesses	DaimlerChrysler
organizations	American Heart Association
unions	Teamsters
schools	University of Memphis
religious figures	the Blessed Virgin
religions	Buddhism
sacred books	the Bible, the Torah
place names	Asia, France
geographic features	the Gulf of Mexico
buildings	the Empire State Building
structures	Jacob's Field
monuments	the Alamo
ships and planes	S.S. *Titanic,* Boeing 767
automobiles	Mercedes ML320
documents	the Constitution
cultural movements	Romanticism, Vorticism
historical periods	Pax Romana, Victorian Age

days and months	Wednesday, June
holidays	Halloween, Fourth of July
course titles	History 101
paintings and sculptures	*Guernica,* the *Venus de Milo*
brand names	Kleenex, Coke

Capitalize words like *river, park, street,* and *road* only when they refer to a specific road, river, or street.

Georgetown Road	a gravel road
the Mississippi River	an American river

Do not capitalize seasons or compass directions unless they are being used as a place name.

winter, spring
north, south
North America, the South

Capitalize adjectives formed from proper names.

Palestinian history   Martian expedition

Capitalize abstractions to give them special emphasis. Compare the two examples.

What is this thing called Love?
Adil had fallen in love again.

Capitalize all letters in most acronyms.

OPEC   NATO treaty

b Abbreviations

Be consistent in punctuating abbreviations and acronyms.

- Abbreviations of single words usually take periods: vols., Jan., Mr.
- Abbreviations spoken letter by letter are usually written without periods: HBO, IRS, CNN.
- Acronyms spoken as complete words do not require periods: CARE, NATO, NOW.
- Periods are usually omitted after abbreviations in technical writing unless an item might be misread without the period: *ft* for *foot, km* for *kilometer,* but *in.* for *inch.*

Be consistent in capitalizing abbreviations and acronyms.
Capitalize the following.

- Abbreviations of words that are capitalized when written out: General Motors—GM; 98° Fahrenheit—98°F. But do not capitalize abbreviations of words not capitalized when written out: pound—lb; minutes—min.
- Most acronyms: IRS, CRT, NVC.
- B.C. and A.D. or B.C.E. and C.E.

Ordinarily, *a.m.* and *p.m.* appear in lowercase, although uppercase is acceptable.

Use the appropriate abbreviations for titles, academic degrees, and names.   Some titles are almost always abbreviated (Mr., Ms., Mrs., Jr.). Others are normally written out, although these may be abbreviated when they precede a first name or initial.

Professor Campbell	Prof. Kermit Campbell
Reverend Eagle	Rev. Ann Eagle

Use appropriate common abbreviations.   The following are appropriate in all types of writing.

businesses	IBM, A&P, MTV
organizations	NCAA, GOP
time	43 B.C.E., A.D. 2005
temperature	13°C, 98°F
places	Washington, D.C.

The following abbreviations are appropriate in special situations, such as technical reports, footnotes, recipes, forms, and addresses. In most writing, however, the terms should be written out in full.

months	Jan., Aug.
days	Mon., Fri.
time	60 mins., 3 hrs.
weights	30 lb, 29 kg
measures	3 tsp, 26 km
book terms	p., vol., ch.
states (postal)	CA, NY, TX, WI

Some abbreviations should be used only with numerals.

Sales were 100 percent on target.
or
Sales were 100% on target.

Abbreviate common Latin terms such as *et cetera (etc.)* and *et alia (et al.).* Although these terms often appear in footnotes, use them sparingly in most formal writing. Check stylebooks to see which abbreviations are preferred in a given field.

c Numbers

Write out numbers from one to nine; use numerals for numbers larger than nine. Note, however, that MLA style recommends spelling out any number that can be expressed in one or two words.

thirteen   twenty-one   three hundred

Combine words and figures for large round numbers.

100 billion   432 million

Use numerals appropriately.

addresses	1900 East Blvd.
dates	July 4, 1776
exact amounts of money	$3.43
measurements	2.5 miles, 33°C
page and chapter numbers	page 43, Chapter 6
percentages	75 percent
scores	a 6–2 victory
statistics	average test score 530, median income $33,000
time	10:00 a.m., 2:15 p.m. (but ten in the morning, six o'clock)

Don't begin sentences with numerals. Either spell out the number or rephrase the sentence so that the numeral is not the first word.

Thirty-two
~~32~~ people were standing in line.

When two separate numbers occur together, write one out and use a numeral for the other.

three
The country acquired ~~3~~ 100-million-dollar loans.

Spell out ordinal numbers: first, second, third, fourth, and so on. Don't make these words adverbs by adding *-ly*.

The ~~1st~~ *first* thing we had to do was bait our hooks.

Second~~ly~~, we had to learn how to cast.

34 Spelling, Dictionary, Thesaurus

"My spelling is Wobbly. It's good spelling but it Wobbles, and the letters get in the wrong places."

—A. A. MILNE, humorist and
children's author

EXPRESS!

Readers react very strongly to spelling errors, so carefully edit the final draft of any paper you write. Most spelling errors involve simple words rather than difficult ones, and the toughest errors to catch are habitual ones, such as mistaking *their* for *there* and *to* for *too*.

To track your spelling trouble spots, keep a file—on disk or on paper—of the words you frequently misspell. Check your final draft against your list before you print out the final copy of your paper.

a Spelling

Proofread carefully to eliminate obvious errors. Here are three effective proofreading techniques.

Read a draft slowly, aloud.
Read a draft with a pencil in hand; touch each word as you read.
Read a draft backward to isolate individual words.

Be especially careful of words that contain the following elements.

- Words that contain *ei* or *ie*: receive, believe, foreign, counterfeit
- Words with silent letters: pneumonia, debt, answer
- Words that end in suffixes

  -able or *-ible:* laughable, visible
  -ance or *-ence*: guidance, obedience
  -ant or *-ent*: attendant, different
  -cede, -ceed, or *-sede:* precede, proceed, supersede

- Words that contain double consonants: occurrence, embarrass, exaggerate, accumulate, accommodate, recommend
- Contractions: who's, it's, you're, don't, won't, can't (see pages 219–220)
- Possessive forms: Jones's, Boz's (see page 219)
- Hyphenated words: double-edged, mothers-in-law (see pages 224–225)

Eliminate errors that result from problems with pronunciation or misreading. You may not recognize some spelling errors until a reader points them out. The following list gives some examples of words to look for.

Incorrect	Correct
alot	a lot
alright	all right
arguement	argument
athelete	athlete
beleive	believe
definately	definitely
enviroment	environment
Febuary	February
goverment	government
hankerchief	handkerchief
knowlege	knowledge
mispell	misspell
neccesary	necessary
noticable	noticeable
occured	occurred
perscription	prescription
privlege	privilege
recieve	receive
roomate	roommate

(continued)

Incorrect	Correct
seperate	separate
supposadly	supposedly
suprise	surprise
surpress	suppress
temperture	temperature
truely	truly

When in doubt, look up the spellings of words. As you write, mark doubtful spellings and consult a dictionary after you've drafted a section of your paper. Avoid spellings labeled chiefly British, archaic, or obsolete unless you have a special reason for using them, such as a direct quotation.

Apply spelling rules—if helpful. Spelling rules in English tend to be complicated, hard to remember, and unreliable. Guidelines such as those below can help, but they never cover every exception.

- Choosing between *ei* and *ie*. In general, *i* comes before *e* except after *c*—unless *ei* has a long "*a*" sound.

  believe   eight

  receive   weigh

  Significant exceptions weaken even this familiar guideline.

  counterfeit   either

  weird   foreign

- Adding prefixes. Prefixes do not change the spelling of the stem word.

Incorrect	Correct
mispelled	misspelled
unecessary	unnecessary
dissappear	disappear

- Doubling consonants in suffixes. Generally, double consonants when adding suffixes to a one-syllable word that ends in one vowel plus a consonant.

  hit   hitting

  swim   swimming

  Double consonants if the word ends in a vowel and a consonant and the final syllable before the suffix is stressed once the suffix has been added.

  occur   occurred   occurrence

  refer   referred

begin	beginning
control	controlling

Don't double consonants if some other syllable is stressed once the suffix has been added.

refer	reference
accustom	accustomed

Don't double consonants if the syllable before the suffix contains more than one vowel or ends in more than one consonant.

speed	speeding
bank	banking

Dropping final *e*'s before suffixes. Drop a final silent *e* if the suffix begins with a vowel.

slide	sliding
arrange	arranging
refute	refutable

Do not drop the final *e* if the main word ends in *c* or *g* and the suffix begins with *a*; doing so causes the preceding *c*'s and *g*'s to have a hard sound, as in *cook* and *gun*.

Incorrect	**Correct**
replacable	replaceable
changable	changeable

Do not drop a final silent *e* if the suffix begins with a consonant.

bereave	bereavement
hate	hateful

- Adding suffixes to words ending in *y*. Change *y* to *i* after a consonant.

merry	merriment
fancy	fanciful

Do not change *y* to *i* in one-syllable words.

pry	prying
play	playing

Do not change *y* to *i* after a vowel or in proper names.

employ	employing
Alice Petry	the Petrys

- Pay close attention to homonyms—words that sound or
  look alike. These words cause many errors because they are
  easily confused. As with other difficult words, build a list of
  your habitual troublemakers. Here is a list of some common
  troublemakers.

Homonyms

all ready (set to go)   already (by now)

altar (table)   alter (change)

bare (empty, clear)   bear (carry)

board (group/plank/   bored (uninterested)
climb on)

brake (stop)   break (fracture)

capital (seat of   capitol (government
government)   building)

cite (point out)   sight (see)   site (location)

complement (make   compliment (praise)
complete)

council (group)   counsel (advice/lawyer)

desert (abandon/   dessert (treat)
arid place)

gorilla (large ape)   guerrilla (soldier)

hear (perceive sound)   here (this place)

its (possessive)   it's (contraction for *it is*)

lead (to direct/metal)   led (past tense of *to lead*)

lessen (decrease)   lesson (instruction)

passed (went by/met   past (what's occurred)
standards)

patience (tolerance)   patients (people under
medical care)

peace (harmony)   piece (part or portion)

principal (head of   principle (standard/
school/most   moral guide)
important)

road (highway)   rode (past tense of *ride*)

stationary (not   stationery (writing
moving)   material)

their (possessive)   there (in that place)   they're
(contraction
for *they are*)

threw (past tense of *throw*)	through (across)
throne (royal seat)	thrown (past participle of *throw*)
weak (not strong)	week (seven days)
wear (to have on)	where (place)
weather (climate)	whether (if/choice)
whose (possessive)	who's (contraction for *who is*)
your (possessive)	you're (contraction for *you are*)

- Spell plurals correctly. Add *-s* to most nouns to form the plural.

toy	toys
picture	pictures
demonstration	demonstrations

Add *-es* when the plural adds a syllable to the pronunciation of a noun. This occurs most often with words ending in *-s, -sh, -ch, -z,* or *-x*.

dish	dishes
summons	summonses
arch	arches
hex	hexes

Learning some general guidelines will help you spot troublesome cases.

- Recognize common irregular plurals, such as *man/men; woman/women;* and *mouse/mice*.
- Learn common plural patterns.

Consonant + *-y* = *-ies*

family	families
party	parties

Consonant + *-o* = *-oes*

hero	heroes
tomato	tomatoes

Vowel + *-o* = | ***-os*** |

video	videos
patio	patios

-f* =** | ***-ves |

thief	thieves
scarf	scarves

- Check the plural of compound words, especially if they are hyphenated expressions. Usually the first word in the compound is pluralized.

attorney general	attorneys general
father-in-law	fathers-in-law
passerby	passersby

e-TIPS

A spelling checker on a word processor will find misspelled words—as long as the mistakes aren't legitimate words on their own. For example, a spelling checker will signal if you spell *supposed* as "suposed" but not if you've omitted the *d* at the end of the word, because *suppose* is a correctly spelled word by itself.

After you've run the spelling checker, proofread the draft again to find errors computers don't catch, such as homonyms and usage errors.

b Dictionary and Thesaurus

Own a desk-sized dictionary.   Desk or collegiate dictionaries typically contain enough entries for most routine writing jobs.

Consult an unabridged dictionary when necessary.   When you are looking for a rare, obscure, or old word, or when you need comprehensive or historical information about a term, consult an unabridged dictionary, routinely available in the library reference room. The *Oxford English Dictionary* is the most famous unabridged dictionary.

Use a pocket dictionary as a convenience.   Rely on a pocket dictionary for correct spellings and basic meanings. It will contain fewer entries, shorter definitions, and sketchier etymologies (word origins) than do college dictionaries.

Use a thesaurus judiciously.   A *thesaurus* is a dictionary of synonyms (and usually antonyms) to help you find the best word for a particular situation. Be sure that any synonyms you select match both denotatively and connotatively the words you intend to replace.

Glossary of Grammatical Terms

absolute. A phrase that modifies an entire sentence. Absolutes are often infinitive or participial phrases. Unlike other modifying phrases, absolutes do not necessarily modify a word or phrase standing near them.

> **To put it politely,** Connie is irritating.

> She will publish the entire story, **space permitting.**

> **Scripts discarded, props disassembled, costumes locked away in trunks,** the annual Shakespeare festival concluded.

adjective. A word that modifies a noun or pronoun. Some adjectives describe the words they modify, explaining how many, which color, which one, and so on.

> an **unsuccessful** coach   a **green** motel

> the **lucky** one   a **sacred** icon

Such adjectives frequently have comparative and superlative forms.

> the **blacker** cat   the **happiest** people

Other adjectives limit or specify the words they modify.

> **this** adventure   **every** penny

> **each** participant   **neither** video

Proper nouns can also serve as adjectives.

> **Texan** wildlife   **Eisenhower** era

adverb. A word that modifies a verb, an adjective, or another verb. Adverbs explain where, when, and how.

>   adverb   verb
> Bud **immediately** *suspected* foul play at the Hutton mansion.

>   adverb adjective
> It seemed **extremely** *odd* to him that Mrs. Hutton should load a large burlap sack into the trunk of her Mercedes.

>   adverb   adverb
> Mrs. Hutton replied **rather** *evasively* when Bud questioned her about what she was up to.

Some adverbs modify complete sentences.

> **adverb**
> **Obviously,** Mr. Hutton had been murdered!

appositive. A word or phrase that stands next to a noun and modifies it by restating or expanding its meaning. Note that appositives are ordinarily surrounded by commas. (See 28c.)

> Connie Lim, **editor of the paper and a staunch liberal,** was furious when former President Clinton gave his only campus interview to Sue Wesley, **chair of the Young Republicans.**

articles. The words, **the, a,** and **an** used before a noun. **The** is called a **definite article** because it points to something specific: **the** book, **the** church, **the** criminal. **A** and **an** are indefinite articles because they refer more generally: **a** book, **a** church, **a** criminal. (See 25b.)

auxiliary verbs. Verbs, usually some form of *be, do,* or *have,* that combine with other verbs to show various relations of tense, voice, mood, and so on. All the words in boldface are auxiliary verbs: **has** seen, **will be** talking, **would have been** going, **are** investigating, **did** mention, **should** prefer. Auxiliary verbs are also known as helping verbs. (See 26a.)

conjunctions, coordinating. The words *and, or, nor, for, but, yet,* and *so* used to link words, phrases, and clauses that serve equivalent functions in a sentence. A coordinating conjunction is used to join two independent clauses or two dependent clauses.

> Oscar **and** Marie directed the play.
>
> Oscar liked the story, **but** Marie did not.

conjunctions, subordinating. Words or expressions such as *although, because, if, since, before, after, when, even though, in order that,* and *while* that relate subordinate or dependent clauses to independent ones (see 28c). Subordinating conjunctions introduce subordinate clauses.

> **subordinate clause**
> **When** the show opened, audiences stayed away.

gender. A classification of nouns and pronouns as masculine (*actor, muscleman, he*), feminine (*actress, midwife, she*), or neuter (*tree, it*).

gerund. A verb form used as a noun: *smiling, biking, walking.* (See 26b.) Most gerunds end in **-ing** and, consequently, look identical to the present participle.

| GERUND | **Smiling** is good for the health. |
| PARTICIPLE | A **smiling** critic is dangerous. |

However, gerunds function as nouns, while participles act as modifiers. Gerunds usually appear in the present tense, but they can take other forms.

Having been criticized made Brian angry.
gerund in past tense, passive voice, acting as subject of the sentence

Being asked to play an encore was a compliment Otto enjoyed.
gerund in present tense, passive voice, as subject of sentence

infinitive. A verbal that can usually be identified by the word **to** preceding the base form of a verb: *to strive, to seek, to find, to endure*. Infinitives do take other forms to show various tenses and voices: *to be seeking, to have found, to have been found*. Infinitives can act as nouns, adjectives, adverbs, and absolutes (see 26b).

| | **subject** |
| INFINITIVE AS NOUN | **To capture** a market is not easy. |

| | **modifies the noun *posters*** |
| INFINITIVE AS ADJECTIVE | Greta had many posters **to redesign.** |

| | **modifies the verb *laughed*** |
| INFINITIVE AS ADVERB | Mr. Stavros laughed **to forget** his troubles. |

| INFINITIVE AS ABSOLUTE | **To be blunt,** the paper is plagiarized. |

interjection. A word that expresses emotion or feeling, but that is not grammatically part of a sentence. Interjections can be punctuated as exclamations (!) or attached to a sentence with a comma. Interjections include *oh, hey, wow,* and *well.*

modal auxiliary. An auxiliary verb that indicates possibility, necessity, permission, desire, capability, and so on. Modal auxiliaries include *can, could, may, might, will, shall, should, ought,* and *must.* (See 26a.)

Hector **can** write.

Hector **might** write.

Hector **must** write.

noun. A word that names a person, place, thing, idea, or quality. In sentences, nouns can serve as subjects, objects, complements, appositives, and even modifiers.

participle. A verb form that is used as a modifier (see 26a). The present participle ends with **-ing**. For regular verbs, the past participle ends with **-ed**; for irregular verb forms, the form of the past participle will vary. Participles have the following forms.

To Perform (a regular verb)

PRESENT, ACTIVE	performing
PRESENT, PASSIVE	being performed
PAST, ACTIVE	performed
PAST, PASSIVE	having been performed

Participles can serve as simple modifiers.

> modifies *Officer Bricker*
> **Smiling,** Office Bricker wrote the traffic ticket.

However, they often take objects, complements, and modifiers of their own to form verbal phrases, which play an important role in shaping sentences.

> **Writing** the ticket for speeding, Bricker laughed at his own cleverness in catching Arthur.

> **Having been ridiculed** often enough in the past by Arthur, Bricker now had his chance for revenge.

> Arthur, **knowing** what his friends were doing to Officer Bricker's car, smiled as he took the ticket.

Like an infinitive, a participle can also serve as an **absolute**—that is, a phrase that modifies an entire sentence.

> All things **considered,** the prank was worth the ticket.

parts of speech. The eight common categories by which words in a sentence are identified according to what they do, how they are formed, where they are placed, and what they mean. Those basic categories are **nouns, pronouns, adjectives, verbs, adverbs, prepositions, conjunctions,** and **interjections.**

preposition. A word that links a noun or pronoun to the rest of a sentence. Prepositions point out many kinds of basic relationships: *on, above, to, for, in, out, through, by,* and so on. The combination of a preposition and a noun or pronoun produces a **prepositional phrase** such as *on our house, above it, to him, in love, through them, by the garden gate.*

pronoun. A word that acts like a noun but doesn't name a specific person, place, or thing—*I, you, he, she, it, they, whom, who, what, myself, oneself, this, these, that, all, both, anybody,* and so on. (See Chapter 23.)

verb. The word or phrase that establishes the action of a sentence or expresses a state of being. (See Chapter 22.)

                              verb
        The music **played** on.

                                  verb
        Turning the volume down **proved** to be difficult.

A verb and all its auxiliaries, modifiers, and complements is called the **predicate** of a sentence.

        complete subject   predicate
        David's band **would have played throughout the night.**

                complete subject   predicate
        Turning the volume down on the band **proved to be much more difficult than the neighbors had anticipated it might be.**

verbals. Verb forms that act like nouns, adjectives, or adverbs (see Chapter 26). The three kinds of verbals are **infinitives, participles,** and **gerunds.** Like verbs, verbals can take objects to form phrases. But verbals are described as **nonfinite** (that is, "unfinished") verbs because they cannot alone make complete sentences. A complete sentence requires a **finite** verb—that is, a verb that changes form to indicate person, number, and tense.

NONFINITE VERB—INFINITIVE	**To have found** security . . .
FINITE VERB	I **have found** security.
NONFINITE VERB—PARTICIPLE	The actor **performing** the scene . . .
FINITE VERB	The actor **performs** the scene.

Credits and Works Cited

Text and Illustrations

Austin, Jane. "Pride and Prejudice," 1813

Bohrer, Becky. "Grey Wolves Thrive in Mont. After Decade", in The Washington Post, January 10, 2005, as accessed from washingtonpost.com.

Boyer, Ernest L. "Creating the New American College," *The Chronicle of Higher Education,* 1994.

Coles, Robert. *The Moral Life of Children.* New York: Houghton Mifflin, 1986.

Cummings, E.E. From "anyone lived in a pretty how town" from *Complete Poems: 1904–1962* by E.E. Cummings, edited by George J. Firmage. Reprinted by permission of Liveright Publishing Corporation.

Explorer Web Browser, 9 screenshots.

Hairston, Maxine; Ruszkiewicz, John; Friend, Christy. From *Scott Foresman Handbook for Writers, The,* 7th Edition, © 2004. Reprinted by permission of Pearson Education, Inc., Upper Saddle River, NJ.

Hairston, Maxine; Ruszkiewicz, John; Friend, Christy. 2 figures, "Unemployment", from *Scott Foresman Handbook for Writers,* 7th Edition, by John Ruszkiewicz et al (Prentice Hall, 2003), p. 159–160. © 2004. Reprinted by permission of Pearson Education, Inc., Upper Saddle River, NJ.

Johnson, Paul. *Intellectuals.* New York: Harper & Row, Inc. 1988, p. 73.

Roland, Alex. "Leave the People Home," from *USA Today Online,* July 3, 1997. Reprinted by permission of Alex Roland.

Sadker, Myra, and David. *Failing at Fairness: How Our Schools Cheat Girls.* New York: Touchstone Books/Simon & Schuster, 1994.

Stern, Barbara Lang. "Tears Can Be Crucial to Your Physical and Emotional Health," *Vogue,* June 1979, Condé Nast Publications.

Women In Science. Screenshots reprinted by permission of Women In Science

Young, Kathy. "Keeping Women Weak," *NEXT,* Eric Liu, ed. New York: W.W. Norton, 1994.

Photos

2: Gwendolyn Brooks, Corbis/Bettmann; 5: "United We Win" poster, National Archives and Records Administration, Still Picture Branch; 5: Tarot Weisser, "Make Love Not War" poster, Center for the Study of Political Graphics; 10: Alice Walker, Jim Marshall/Harcourt Brace College Publishers; 14: Gene Fowler, Getty Images, Inc—Liaison; 20: Robert Motherwell, Arnold Newman/Getty Images, Inc.; 30: Morris Udall, Owen Franken/ Corbis/Bettmann; 29: Edith Head, Hulton Archive/Getty Images; 49: Caricature of Peter Steiner © Peter Steiner; 51: Albert Einstein, Corbis/Bettmann; 65: David Letterman, Michael Hirsch/Corbis/ Sygma; 70: Sir Julian Huxley, CP Globe Photos, Inc.; 83: Jorge Luis Borges, Magnum Photos, Inc.; 87: Oscar Wilde, Corbis/ Bettmann © Bettmann/Corbis; 90: Barbara Tuchman, Photofest; 96: Eric Hoffer, Getty Images/Time Life Pictures; 102: Miles Davis, Shepard Sherbell Corbis/Bettmann; 108: Samuel Langhorne Clemens (Mark Twain), Corbis/ Bettmann; 111: John Maynard Keynes, Getty Images Inc./Hulton Archive Photos; 116: Benjamin Franklin by Joseph Siffred Duplessis, ca. 1745–1802. Corbis/ Bettmann; 122: Rita Rudner, Lisa Rose/Globe Photos, Inc.; 177: Niels Bohr, AIP/The Bohr Collection/Photo Researchers, Inc.; 179: Larry Bird, Bob Greene/Photofest; 184: John Updike, Agence France Presse (AFP)/Getty Images; 191: Wayne Gretzky, AP Wide World Photos; 201: Lorraine Hansberry, Corbis/Bettmann; 207: Albert Einstein, Dpa/Landov LLC; 210: Ingrid Bengis, Nancy Crampton; 216: Paul Harvey, Reuters/Rose Prouser/Landov LLC; 220: Mistinguette, P. Abers/Culver Pictures, Inc.; 225: Robert Frost, Arnold Newman/Getty Images, Inc.; 229: Ralph Waldo Emerson, Popperfoto/H. Armstrong Roberts; 232: Doug Larson, Ducks Unlimited, Inc.; 235: Lily Tomlin, Getty Images Inc./ Hulton Archive Photos; 244: Carl Sagan, AFP/Newscom; 250: A.A. Milne, author, with child, Popperfoto/H. Armstrong Roberts.

Index

Contents